WE CAN BE KIND♥

Healing Our World
One Kindness at a Time

by David Friedman

Mango Publishing Group
2850 Douglas Road, 3rd Floor
Coral Gables, FL 33134 USA
info@mango.bz

For special orders, quantity sales, course adoptions and corporate sales, please email the publisher at sales@mango.bz. For trade and wholesale sales, please contact Ingram Publisher Services at: customer.service@ingramcontent.com or +1.800.509.4887.

Library of Congress Control Number: 2017955298

Eric Rosswood

We Can Be Kind: Healing Our World One Kindness at a Time

ISBN: (paperback) 978-1-63353-675-3, (ebook) 978-1-63353-676-0

BISAC - SEL021000, SELF-HELP / Motivational & Inspirational
        - OCC019000 BODY, MIND & SPIRIT / Inspiration &
        Personal Growth

Printed in the United States of America

Based on the song
"We Can Be Kind" by David Friedman

Kind: adjective,

1. of a good or benevolent nature or disposition, as a person
2. having, showing, or proceeding from benevolence
3. indulgent, considerate, or helpful; humane (often followed by *to*)
4. mild, gentle

PREFACE

The chapter headings in this book are taken directly from my song "We Can Be Kind," first recorded by Nancy LaMott. Before you read this book, please take a moment to download Nancy's recording of the song by going to https://goo.gl/pZPpbh. It's *free*, as Kindness always is and should be.

Since the purpose of this book is to spread the word about Kindness to the entire world, please feel free to share this URL and your downloaded recording on Facebook, Twitter, with your friends, with your mailing lists, and anywhere you can. And while you're at it, if you enjoy the book, share that too.

Together we can Heal Our World, One Kindness at a Time.

David Friedman

Contents

CHAPTER 17   156

We Must Walk the Walk About It

CHAPTER 18   166

You and I, Do or Die, We've Got To Try to Get Along

CHAPTER 19   173

And Maybe We'll Find True Peace of Mind

CHAPTER 20   180

If We Always Remember,
We Can Be Kind

Epilogue   185

Authors bio   187

Foreword

_____

by Lucie Arnaz

I woke up early this morning determined to write the foreword to this book, but still unsure where to start. As I was pouring a cup of coffee, I heard a *thud* on our kitchen plate glass window. It happens a lot this time of day in the desert; the reflection must tell the birds that the landscape continues in this direction. Then they get a big surprise. I went ahead and made breakfast before sitting down to write and, while at the table finishing my omelet, looked to the window on my left and saw a large patch of smashed feathers. Out the window, on the patio, still on the ground from almost forty-five minutes ago, was a little grey-brown sparrow…sitting upright, perfectly still. I told my husband, Larry, what had happened earlier and that it must have been sitting there this whole time trying to recover from the shock.

You don't know me, but I think I must have been an animal or bird in my last life—because I can't see things like that without wanting to help. We decided to give it some water. I filled a tiny dish and crept out slowly onto the patio, fully expecting the sparrow to scare and take off. It didn't. So, I snuck over, got down on the pavement, and put the little bowl in front of her. (It looked like a female.) She allowed me to do this, to just be there and gently stroke her head and back feathers, many of which had been left on the window. As I lay there with her, I kept thinking, "What else should I or can I do? Nothing. All I can do is help her get through this and protect her from the large hawks that swoop in from time to time to prey on the injured." I sat up with my knees to my chest and decided to wait until she could fly away, and I started to softly sing: *"So many things we can't control. So many hurts that happen every day. So many heartaches that pierce the soul…"* Just then, the bird jumped up onto my knee! She just sat there really looking at me, cocking her head from side to side. It was absolutely magical. I felt it was a kind of "Thank you," and so I said, "Anytime!" She blinked a few more times, fluttered her feathers, and took off over the hedge. *A Course in Miracles* teaches us that "we don't know what anything is for," and that is often true. But I sure know what this was for this morning!

I met David Friedman at the tenth anniversary *Help Is on the Way* benefit concert in San Francisco in August 2004. He was the Special Guest and played his title song to accompany us at the finalé. Near midnight, after all the schmoozing and picture taking was done, Kieth Dodge (my best friend and right arm) and I decided we were starving and didn't want to go to Martuni's for drinks with everyone else, but should just get some food. Pointing at David and his partner, neither of whom we had formally met, Kieth said, "Let's ask them!" Four hours later, we left Lorie's Diner satiated from laughter and exploding with inspiration. The four of us had talked about pretty much everything: *the business we call "show,"* lousy dates, bunions, and spirituality. It turned out that David's partner, Shawn Moninger, was a lighting designer at *Don't Tell Mama* for twenty years and now was a Unity minister! I had always been an enormous fan of David Friedman's music, and to get to sit with him and listen to him recite some of his own lyrics that night—and to have him help me understand where they came from—was unforgettable.

We stayed in contact and visited them in New York City, and they drove out to our home in Westchester. We were honored to now call them friends.

In March of 2006, I was doing a concert at The Ridgefield Playhouse in Connecticut and asked Shawn if he would like to light the show for me and, thankfully, he accepted. (Shawn is responsible for so many kinds of light in my life!) I told David that I was thinking of singing "Help Is on the Way" at this show, since my pal Kieth had passed tragically and unexpectedly a few months before. We were all still reeling from the loss, and I couldn't think of a better song to move us through that pain. Then I got really ballsy and asked David whether he would play the piano for me if I sang it. He immediately agreed. But since I had never performed the song in public, David suggested I might perhaps like to sing it for the congregation at Shawn's Sunday service at Unity in Norwalk, Connecticut. Again, David said he would play for me; this would be a kind of practice run for Kieth's memorial concert. But I was skeptical: *"Sing in a church?!"* David replied, "Well, it's more like a lounge in Vegas with a great takeaway message." It scared me. I have long considered myself a "recovering Catholic" with no friendly relationship to "religion," but I said I would take a chance. As I sat there that Sunday morning in the lovely "Unity lounge" above the Ford dealership in Norwalk, Connecticut, waiting to do my song, I listened to what Shawn had to say about

Spirit and Life and Truth and who knows what else, and I found myself suddenly and uncontrollably dissolved in tears. Whatever it was, it was something I really needed to hear. Just then I heard David say the words: "We're on!" Oh, great.

The Ridgefield concert was a huge success, and David's song stole the show. Friends were popping up from within the audience, singing parts of the refrain: *"Help is on the way...From places you don't know about today... From friends you may not have met, yet...Believe me when I say...I know Help is on the way."* It was all true for me. And it was extremely moving.

And I kept coming back to Unity. For Shawn's talks. For the "Thought Exchange" classes that David teaches each week. For the summer retreats. To study *A Course in Miracles.* To learn what prayer really is. To finally feel connected to an all-encompassing God I knew I didn't have to fear.

Unity and its teachings continue to spiritually feed my soul. And David's unique take on circumstances, his Divinely inspired understanding of why we respond in certain ways to things that happen to us, has been my daily go-to "tool box" for eleven years. Over these years, I have gone through numerous challenging circumstances, large and small: a crisis with one of our five children, health issues, my relationship with my husband, a career challenge, even just road rage. In times like these, David has helped me to come at things from a place where you can heal from—and he can help you too. David's process of "Thought Exchange" is a flawless remedy for those times when whatever "it" is won't just roll off your back. (To learn more about Thought Exchange, go to thethoughtexchange.com.)

And now with *We Can Be Kind*, David has taken some of his most humanity-cleansing lyrics and broken them down for us so we can better understand how we're all meant to behave here on this planet. Even by floating the displeasing idea that "being kind" is something that we might not be doing, David is still teaching us a positive lesson. For a minute when we hear the song, we have to think, "Wait a minute, you mean I'm *not*?!" No. We are really not always very kind—not to ourselves, nor to those who pass our way. Being kind to yourself is the first thing to learn, and one of the *only* specific life instructions I remember from my mother. She always used to say to me,

"Be kind to Lucie," as if "Lucie" were someone almost other than myself. Now I understand what she meant. If you don't take care of your own sanity, health, and well-being, you cannot expect to be able to care for anyone else. We have to learn to love and forgive ourselves before we can know what love feels like when we see it elsewhere. And today, with the immediate, faceless, instant gratification of "commenting" on social media and some of the just plain meanness we see coming from those in leadership positions, we are forgetting what being kind even sounds like. This wonderful book puts that all back into perspective. It reminds us *how* we can actually *be* kind and *do* kinder things…and why that even matters.

I read this book in a day. I could not put it down. Like everything David writes, it sounds exactly the way he talks. And, because of that, it's wonderfully witty and accessible.

There is no greater time for this message to be heard, and no better person to be delivering it. Thank you, David.

—Lucie Arnaz

Introduction

Kindness has always held a very special and unique place in my heart and mind, because Kindness is something we can *always* choose. We can't always feel loving toward someone, but we can *always* choose to be kind toward them. We can't always choose not to feel irritated or angry, but we can *always* choose to be Kind, even when we are not feeling kindly toward them. We can't always solve a problem, but we can *always* choose to be Kind while trying to solve it or while being with the fact that we can't. We can't always agree with one another on politics or matters of taste, but we can *always* choose to be Kind as we discuss these things. We may not have the financial or physical wherewithal to contribute to a cause that needs our support, but one way in which we can *always* contribute is that We Can Be Kind. The other wonderful, all-encompassing thing about Kindness is that any time we do make a positive contribution to a situation, whether it be with action, money, or some other type of gift, the contribution is, by definition, a demonstration of a way in which we are being Kind.

We Can Be Kind

As a songwriter, I've always been aware that I do not write my songs, they write me. When someone asks me, "How do you write a song?" I usually answer, "I have no idea how to write a song. But I do know how to open myself up in a way that makes it extremely possible that a song will write itself through me. This being the case, I usually don't know everything there is to know about the songs I write. Often, my songs contain wisdom or information that I myself don't have but, rather, that I need to hear or learn.

Of all the songs I've ever written (or, to be more precise, that have ever written me), the song I'm most grateful for is "We Can Be Kind." The late, great Nancy LaMott was the first person to record this song (I wrote it especially for her), and every time I listen to her recording or hear any number of the other wonderful singers who have recorded it or sung it live, I find myself hearing the song in new and different ways that help deepen my understanding of what Kindness is and how I can practice it. In fact, I've always felt that if there was just one song of mine that I hoped the whole world would hear, it would definitely be "We Can Be Kind."

So, when I was asked to write a book about Kindness, I thought: "Why not go through the song 'We Can Be Kind' line by line, explore the meaning of each line, tell some stories and some personal history that relate to the line, and then offer ways in which we can be kind not only to others but to ourselves by applying the lessons each line has to teach us?" In the process of writing this book, I learned a lot, not only about myself, but about what Kindness means and about how to practice it in each and every moment of my day-to-day life, in order to help and heal not only myself but everyone with whom I come into contact. Hence the title of this book: *We Can Be Kind, Healing Our World One Kindness at a Time.*

I sincerely hope that as you read this book and listen to the song "We Can Be Kind" on which it is based, you will not only take in the lessons of the stories I tell and the suggestions I make for how to be kind to yourself and others, but will also remember your own stories and create your own ways to be kind. And I hope you will continue to refer to the book and the song, and that it will inspire you to always be a part of an ever-expanding consciousness of Kindness until it becomes the consciousness of the whole world.

Since the day Nancy LaMott recorded "We Can Be Kind," it has become an anthem for raising awareness and financial support for charitable organizations and social causes all over the world. With this book and CD, I hope to reach a wider audience with the message that no matter what the circumstance, no matter what the problem, we *always* have a choice. We Can Be Kind. And choosing to be kind makes all the difference.

"We Can Be Kind"
Words & Music by David Friedman
sung by Nancy LaMott

So many things we can't control
So many hurts that happen every day
So many heartaches that pierce the soul
So much pain that won't ever go away
How do we make it better?
How do we make it through?
What can we do when there's nothing we can do?

We can be Kind
We can take care of each other
We can remember that deep down inside we all need
the same thing
And maybe we'll find
If we are there for each other
That together we'll weather whatever tomorrow may
bring
Nobody really wants to fight
Nobody really wants to go to war
Everyone wants to make things right
So what are we always fighting for?
Does nobody want to see it?
Does nobody understand?
The power to heal is right here in our hand

We can be Kind
We can take care of each other
We can remember that deep down inside we all need
the same thing
And maybe we'll find
If we are there for each other
That together we'll weather whatever tomorrow
may bring

And it's not enough to talk about it
Not enough to sing a song
We must walk the walk about it
You and I, do or die
We've got to try to get along

We can be Kind
We can take care of each other
We can remember that deep down inside we all need
the same thing
And maybe we'll find
If we are there for each other
That together we'll weather whatever tomorrow
may bring

And maybe we'll find
True peace of mind
If we always remember
We Can Be Kind

CHAPTER 1

So Many Things We Can't Control

As much as we like to think we are in control, and as much as we try to control things, in truth we really have very little control in many areas of our lives. There are constantly things happening in the world at large—in the economy, in other countries, in politics—that affect our lives but which we cannot control. We have no control over sudden illness or unforeseen accidents. We have no control over what other people do or say. As we learn in twelve-step programs, we can't control another person's drinking or addiction to food or spending. We don't control the weather, we don't control the rising and setting of the sun, we don't control storms or natural disasters, and we don't control the forces of the universe, most of which we're not even aware. We don't control the functioning of many of our internal organs, or the multitude of body processes that happen automatically beneath the level of our consciousness. (In fact, I'm often grateful that I don't have to control those. Imagine having to think about how fast your heart has to beat in order to run a certain distance, or how many digestive enzymes you need to secrete to digest the meal you just ate. That would be totally crazy-making.) So when we think about it, unless we can come to terms with the fact that there is so much we can't control, it could be quite frightening to realize that we go through life having so little control over so many things.

Giving Up Control

Whenever I hear someone say, "I finally decided to give up control," my response is always, "You had it?" In looking at my own life, I've realized that situations that seem to cause me the biggest problems involve circumstances in which I feel I don't have control. Not only that, but in looking more deeply, I've realized that the problem is not so much that I don't have control but that I think I should have control, and I try to get control of things I can't control.

A few years ago, a combination of stressful events and lifetime of physical tension caused me to lose my voice.

Being a composer and a public speaker, my voice is my bread and butter, so naturally I was extremely concerned. In an effort to get my voice back, I took all sorts of lessons and did all sorts of therapies, all to no avail. One day, a brilliant voice therapist pointed out to me that my voice knows how it works and I don't, so I needed to get out of its way and let it correct itself. This seemed scary, since I wasn't "doing" the fixing, but it was only when I dared to let go of my futile efforts to control something I couldn't possibly control that I let the part of me that knows how to control it (my unconscious) take over, and my voice was restored. In effect, rather than having to *learn* how to speak and sing, I had to *forget* how to speak and sing so that those parts of me that I could not control could show me. This was being kind to myself. Rather than beating myself up, I let go and connected with the part of me that knew how to solve the problem. It's always there. We just have to let ourselves get out of the way enough to allow it to work.

Guilt and Shame

To me, guilt and shame are the same thing. They are our attempts to have the present be different than it is, or to have the past be different than it was. So many of us waste so much time trying to have had a better childhood. We try to control other people when it is our very own thoughts that are drawing their particular behavior into our lives. Over and over, we find ourselves repeating self-defeating patterns and looking outside ourselves to try to fix something "out there." The only place to ever fix something is inside ourselves. When we can stop trying to control the outside world, we get in touch with the only thing we can control…our thoughts and our internal reactions. Choosing thoughts of guilt and shame is a way in which we are very unkind to ourselves. We keep ourselves trapped in the idea that we are bad, that we are to blame, and that something could and should have been different. The kind thing to do, as painful as it may be, is to see things as they were and as they are. This is where the healing happens.

A Power Greater Than Ourselves

Admitting we can't control something is often the first step to getting in touch with sources of power and information that are not available to us when we are busy trying to use just what we already know to try and make things turn out the way we want them to, even when that might be impossible. When we can simply admit that we are powerless to control a situation or another person, we open the door to other sources of power. Some might call that power God. Some call it Spirit. Some call it Intuition, Inspiration, or Acceptance. Sayings like "Let Go and Let God" and "It's All Good" often give us a new freedom to relax and open to previously unnoticed or unthought-of sources of solutions and support. Sometimes the support or information we need shows up in the form of other people, or Synchronicities occur that we might not have noticed if we were too busy fighting for control. Every one of these things gives us the chance to possibly see the same situation in a different light. I once had a therapist who said to me, "I could tell you something for years and you wouldn't get it, and one day you're sitting next to someone on the bus and they say the exact same thing to you and suddenly you get it." So perhaps, rather than considering circumstances in which we don't have control to be "bad" things, we can look at them as opportunities to expand our base of power and support in ways we might never have imagined.

🐖 We Can Be Kind to Ourselves 🐖

Today, rather than fighting or railing against what you can't control, see if you can simply notice it. When something happens and you realize that you are powerless to do anything about it, instead of going into action, try sitting still and being with the fact that you can't control it. Accept it. Allow it to be as it is. And then notice what happens when you do that. Notice if you begin to feel a sense of peace or if you get more anxious. Whatever it is you feel, don't fight it. Just be with it and see where it leads you. Notice if new ideas you never thought of come to mind. Notice if things happen that you didn't expect. Notice if it becomes OK to have things be just the way they are without your having to fight to change them. In being accepting of the way things are and of yourself as you are, you are not only opening the door to expanded possibilities and unthought-of solutions, but you are reducing your stress and frustration levels. In this way, you are being kind to yourself. And being kind to yourself is the first step in being able to be kind to others.

❧ We Can Be Kind in the World ❧

1. The next time someone says something to you that annoys you, rather than retaliating or trying to change or control them, simply listen to them and let them know that you hear them. Watch how the tone of the conversation changes, and how their ability to hear you expands.

2. The next time someone cuts you off on the road, rather than hitting the horn or swearing at them, try doing nothing or even smiling or waving them on. Their uncontrollable action may have escalated your upset. See what happens, both in their reaction and inside of yourself, when you exhibit kindness by not escalating their action.

3. If you're dealing with an addict or alcoholic who is out of control, it is often important to not respond to them and not help them. This may seem counterintuitive,

but it is often the kindest thing you can do in that you are giving them the opportunity to hit bottom and find their own inner strength, which most likely is the only way they can truly heal.

CHAPTER 2

So Many Hurts That Happen Every Day

OK. There are the things I spoke about in the first chapter that come from out of the blue and are unusual, unexpected, and often shocking. But when we look at our lives, there are also definitely a great number of hurts that happen every day: people speaking to us in a harsh tone, disappointments, missing a train or a bus or a plane, being stuck in traffic, someone bumping into you while you're walking in the street, ongoing financial or health problems, being put on hold for a half-hour, a service person or a customer being rude, having a disagreement with your husband, wife, family, or friends, dealing with someone who has a different political position than you do, trying to lose weight, being jealous of someone or angry at them, and so on. The list of things, many of which occur daily, goes on and on. In fact, one of these is the reason I wrote the song "We Can Be Kind" in the first place.

A Small Incident Inspires a Universal Song

There was an annual benefit event in New York City called *In Celebration of Life*, where composers were paired up with singers. The composers were each asked to write a new song that in some way pertained to healing, and the singers performed these songs in a concert that was given at St. Paul's Cathedral. The AIDS crisis was in full swing, so many of the songs that were written and performed had to do with AIDS. Now if anything qualified as something devastating that could not be controlled, it was AIDS. People across the world were getting sick and dying, and nobody seemed to know anything about how the disease could be cured. In their helplessness, people expressed themselves in whatever ways they could. They talked about it. They sang about it. They raised money for research. What that evening did, alongside so many other performances, research projects, books, speeches, etc., was raise consciousness and open people's minds to the idea that there had to be a cure. By becoming vocal about it, more and more people became open to this idea. The disease was no less terrifying, but these community expressions gave people hope and the sense that they were not alone.

Each year, the concert closed with Nancy LaMott singing a new song I had written for her. This particular year, I asked Nancy what she wanted me to write about, and she said, "I was getting on the bus this morning, and this woman in front of me was so nasty! Could you write a song about how people should be nicer to each other?" And so, out of that little incident, out of one of those "little" hurts that happen every day, I wrote this song which has ended up being sung around the world for all sorts of causes, big and small.

☁ We Can Be Kind to Ourselves ☁

When you notice that something hurtful has happened, see if you can simply register that it has happened and allow yourself to feel however you feel about it. Don't fight it off. Don't try to change it. Often, when hurtful things happen, if we don't try to fight them off or change them, we get to get in touch with painful feelings we've had for a long time which we haven't allowed ourselves to feel and process. This can be, in its own way, very healing. So before you go into action, try being kind to your "Inner Child" by being with it, giving it a chance to feel whatever it feels, and acknowledging that that feeling exists. Kindness is what our Inner Child didn't get in the areas in which it's still in pain. It is you and you alone who can offer this "Inner Child" the kindness it needs to heal.

🍂 We Can Be Kind in the World 🍂

1. When someone in a store, in a bank, or on the street is nasty to you, see what happens if you are not nasty in return. Try to get past their behavior to see why they might be behaving that way. Are they scared? Are they angry? And then, try to offer them what you think they might need to feel better.

2. You may not be able to prevent people from doing things that hurt you, but you certainly can prevent yourself from doing things that hurt others. The next time you find yourself about to do something that might hurt someone, *don't!* Be kind instead and watch what happens, to them as well as inside yourself.

3. Before you speak or act in any given situation, stop for a moment and think: "Am I hurting anyone by doing this?" And if you find that the action you're about to

take or the words you're about to use would be hurtful to someone, see if you can substitute kind actions or words instead.

CHAPTER 3

So Many Heartaches That Pierce the Soul

Heartaches that pierce the soul. Losing a loved one. Losing a pet. Oh my goodness, is that a tough one for so many people. Having a lifelong dream or an important project fall through. Losing one's home or one's job. Having to take care of an ailing parent day after day, or year after year, knowing that they're failing and feeling helpless to heal them. Seeing people discriminated against. Dealing with someone who has a challenging chronic or terminal illness. Getting a diagnosis. Grappling with depression, anxiety, mental illness, or a serious injury. These are all heartaches that happen to so many of us at different times, and which truly do pierce us, testing our fortitude, hampering our ability to be positive and appreciate life, and challenging our Faith, whatever it may be.

Taking the Risk of Loving after Loss

When Nancy LaMott died, she left behind a four-month-old Himalayan Kitten named Mercer. My partner at the time and I decided to take her in. I had never had a cat, and Mercer was quite an imperious purebred Himalayan. As a friend of mine used to say, "She's a great beauty and she knows it." Mercer lived for almost nineteen years and was a comforting constant through my breakup with my partner and through many highs and lows that occurred during that period. She was always there, and I grew to love her deeply. When I met my current partner a few years later, he wasn't so keen on Mercer, but as the years went by, he too developed a great love for her. And then, as inevitably happens, the heartache that pierced our souls occurred. Mercer passed at a ripe old age. As my partner put it, "I had no idea how much Mercer's presence filled our house. It's only now that she's gone that I realize there was not a moment when I thought about our home during the day when I didn't think about where Mercer was."

I was reluctant to get another cat, but my partner pressed me. After a reasonable mourning period, we stumbled across a breeder who had posted a photograph of the most gorgeous Flame Point Himalayan we had ever seen. We went up to meet the kitty, and she was beautiful beyond our wildest dreams—both in the way she looked and in her temperament. We took her home and named her Shmooshie.

A few days after we got her, we took Shmooshie to the vet and he couldn't believe how gorgeous and loving she was. He examined her, told us everything looked good, and then took her temperature. It was 104.3! Something was very wrong. Things went downhill quickly. It turned out that Shmooshie had a disease called FIP which was almost always fatal. We tried everything, but a month later we had to put this beautiful kitten down. We were heartbroken. I swore that I would never go through this again. My soul was indeed pierced.

My partner, however, really wanted another cat. The breeder still had Shmooshie's brother available and offered to give him to us. He had had him tested and he did not show any signs of the FIP virus. I looked at a picture of the cat and wasn't impressed. In hindsight, there's no way I could have been impressed by any cat, because I was too closed down to even think about having another one.

My partner, however, kept pressing me, so finally I relented, saying, "OK. If you really want a cat, he can be your cat. I doubt that I'll ever bond with him, but if you want him, you can take care of him, be responsible for him, and he'll be your cat." So we went up to take a look at Gabriel. When we arrived in the driveway of the breeder's home, I saw Gabriel through a basement window. He was on a table where the breeder was grooming him. My first thought was, "He's so *big*!" He was much bigger than Shmooshie. We went down to the basement and sat down at the table where he was being dried from his bath. Gabriel looked at me across the table, wriggled out of the breeder's arms, walked across the table and kissed me on the nose. Well that was it! I was in love, and we took Gabriel home and he proved to be the most loving, deep-as-a-pool spiritual cat I've ever known.

After a while we decided we wanted a companion for Gabriel. Our breeder had a little white kitten who was like a cotton ball. We fell in love with her and brought her home. And within a month, she too was dead from FIP. Anyone who has a beloved pet knows the intense pain of putting down these beautiful, loving beings. And we had done so three times in one year.

We realized that the two cats that had died had both been very young, and in doing research we found out that if FIP is going to strike, it's usually a kitten who succumbs.

Our breeder had another cat who was almost four years old and had had a few litters, but because of her small size finally had to be spayed. Gwendolyn was very skittish and suspicious, as well as being imperious and beautiful as Mercer had been. But when we took her home, we fell in love with her, and more importantly, Gabriel fell in love with her and welcomed her into our home, constantly cleaning her, hanging around with her, and definitely bonding with her.

So now we had two cats. A Blue Point and a Torti Point. Both Himalayans. My partner decided he wanted a White Flame Point like Shmooshie had been, and sure enough, our breeder had one who, for reasons having to do with his shyness, was not a good breeder (although he was a show champion) and had to be isolated. It was so sad to see Cooper having to live behind a gate in the basement. He had tried to breed once and a female cat had ripped out a lot of his hair. We fell in love with him and took him home. He hid under the bed for two weeks. But you could see Gwendolyn and Gabriel plotting as to how they were going to bring him out. Sometimes Gwendolyn would wait outside the bedroom while Gabriel went in alone to hang out with Cooper under the bed. It was almost like the two cats had consulted with each other and had decided on a strategy.

It's now several years since Mercer's death, and we certainly have gone through soul-piercing heartaches with several cats, but as I look back, I'm so grateful that my partner persisted. The love that these animals bring to our home—the way they greet us as well as guests at the door, the way one sleeps on my partner's head (and cleans it most mornings) while the other sleeps on my arm and the third (Gwendolyn, who is still the most independent) sporadically and graciously gifts us with her presence by curling up between the pillows—is an unbridled experience of pure love for us. We endured the heartache, and so much love came out of it.

GABRIEL

GWENDOLYN

COOPER

🍂 We Can Be Kind to Ourselves 🍂

When we can be with heartaches, recognize them, and feel them, we can more easily acknowledge that we are part of the human race. And that acknowledgement lets us know that we are not alone. Everyone has heartaches, and as we become more empathetic to our own, we become more empathetic to other people's challenges. We more readily identify with other people's challenges, and more easily are able to understand them and be with them. Quietly being with our own heartaches and allowing ourselves to feel them deeply allows us to be human, allows us to heal, and allows us to move forward. This is being kind to ourselves.

🍂 We Can Be Kind in the World 🍂

1. When you see someone who is experiencing heartache, rather than trying to fix it, simply offer them kindness by visiting them, listening to them, and letting them express their pain to your listening ears and heart. Being with them, while understanding that they need to go through what they need to go through to heal

and grow, and not trying to take that experience away from them, is being kind.

2. When you are experiencing heartache, see if there's some way that you can find to be kind to someone else. In this way, even in your darkest hour, you still have something to give. Kindness. Watch what comes back to you.

3. There's a Buddhist tradition called Tonglen in which, when you are experiencing great pain, rather than focusing on yourself, you think of all the other people in the world who are experiencing or have experienced the same pain as you. In this way you convert pain into compassion. When you do this, not only do you find yourself not feeling so alone, but it gives you the opportunity to find someone who is experiencing the same pain as you and get out of yourself by offering them the kindness you would like to receive.

CHAPTER 4

So Much Pain That Won't Ever Go Away

Pain is a fact of life. We may be temporarily free from pain, we may certainly experience great joy, but we are never invulnerable to the possibility of painful experiences. Some of us are in chronic physical pain and though we fight to not have it, sometimes we have to go in the other direction and accept it as a daily fact of life. A parent who has a child with a serious health challenge never has a day where they are not worried or concerned about how their child is doing, how their child is feeling, and whether the child's life can be made better. Then there are, of course, the exigencies of life: anxiety, fears about death, illness, money, success, and so on. Pain is certainly a big part of our lives, whether we choose to notice it or not.

Good Morning Heartache

In the song "Good Morning Heartache," made famous by Billy Holliday, the singer struggles with a heartache that seems to greet her every morning and won't go away. She talks about how she tosses and turns and wrestles with the heartache all night, but it's still there in the morning. She then asks the heartache to stop haunting her, to leave her alone—but her beseeching goes unheard. Ultimately, she gives in, let's go, and says, "Good morning, heartache. Sit down." She acknowledges that there is a pain that will never go away, and telling it to sit down is the first step to being able to be with it, to not resisting it, to starting to come to terms with it. One of the basic tenets of metaphysics is, "What you resist persists." So often we try to fight off pain and it only fights back. When we can stop resisting, we leave room for something different to happen. For insights into what the pain might be about. For the lessons the pain may be teaching us. And again, for solutions we may have never thought of or which, in our resistance, we couldn't see.

"Good Morning, Heartache"
Words & Music by
Dan Fisher, Ervin Drake & Irene Higginbotham

Good morning, heartache, you ol' gloomy sight
Good morning, heartache, thought we'd said goodbye
last night
I turned and tossed until it seemed you had gone
But here you are with the dawn

Wish I'd forget you, but you're here to stay
It seems I met you, when my love went away
Now every day I start by saying to you
Good morning, heartache, what's new?

Stop haunting me now
Can't shake you, no how
Just leave me alone
I've got those Monday blues
Straight through Sunday blues

Good morning, heartache, here we go again
Good morning, heartache, you're the one who knew me
when

Might as well get used to you hangin' around
Good morning, heartache, sit down

❧ We Can Be Kind to Ourselves ❧

To me, the definition of love is unconditionally allowing things to be the way they are. When you love a person unconditionally, your love for them is not based on their being a certain way. You love them no matter what. My partner can be very reactive and get angry when things are upset or disturbed. But it's amazing to watch him with our cats. The cat can climb on a shelf, knock everything off it, and Shawn will say "Oh, honey, that's OK" and pick up the kitty and kiss it. He will never get the things back that were broken, but instead of attacking, he uses it as an opportunity to experience love within himself. Anything, no matter how painful, can be used as an opportunity for love if we approach it with acceptance and allow it to be the way it is. This is unconditional love. This is kindness.

🍂 We Can Be Kind in the World 🍂

1. When you encounter someone who has had a great loss, let them talk to you about it without your commenting or trying to fix it. Just be there. Just listen.

2. When you have done something to hurt someone, rather than explaining or defending yourself, simply apologize for hurting them and let them know you understand why they would be hurt. Even if years later they are still feeling hurt, rather than saying, "When will you get over this?" say, "I know. I hurt you. I will always apologize every time I see that you are still hurt." The hurt may never go away, but if it is simply seen with kindness, the love will be there too. (This is an especially good thing to do in a marriage. People who are able to stay in long, happy relationships usually have this ability.)

3. When someone tells you that they are feeling hopeless or that they have some circumstance that they think will keep them in pain forever, do not try to talk them out of it. The kind thing is to let them know that you know where they are, you hear what they're saying, you are with what they're feeling. This is the kindest way

to allow solutions or at least acceptance and peace of mind to find their way to this person.

CHAPTER 5

How Do We Make It Better?

This is a question we must ask ourselves whenever we encounter a challenging or painful situation. Usually people think of making something better by doing something to get rid of it. But perhaps there are other ways to make the experience of the challenge better other than trying to improve or get rid of the circumstance, especially when it's a circumstance that seems like it can't be improved or changed. Sometimes just being with someone, just "getting" someone, just allowing someone to feel the way they feel is the best thing we can do.

It Only Takes One Word

Years ago, I was having an "argument" with my father about some things he had done when I was younger that had been very upsetting to me. He kept defending himself, trying to explain why he had done what he had done, how I had misperceived the circumstance, and how I should be over it by now. But I kept going at him. Finally, in frustration, he said, "What do you want me to say? Do you want me to apologize? Do you want me to tell you I feel guilty?" My answer was, "No. I just want you to say one word." "And what is that one word?" "The one word I want you to say is, 'Oh.' I don't want you to explain, I don't want you to reason with me, I don't want you to argue with me. I just want you to 'get' where I am and how I feel. There's nothing else to be done.…Just say 'Oh.'"

Don't Fix It, Acknowledge It

A friend of mine was walking with her three-year-old granddaughter, who was wheeling her favorite doll in a baby doll carriage. They came to a staircase, and all of a sudden the carriage fell down the stairs and the doll fell out. The little girl was hysterically crying and seemed inconsolable. My friend, in an effort to make her granddaughter feel better, pointed out that the doll had not been hurt, that everything was fine, that there was nothing to worry about. Still, the little girl screamed. Suddenly, my friend had an insight. She bent down and said to her granddaughter,

"That must have been terribly upsetting to see your doll fall out of the carriage." To which the little girl replied, "Yes, it was." Her grandmother continued, "I can see why you would be crying about this." The little girl said, "Yes," stopped crying, and they went on their merry way and enjoyed the rest of their walk. All her granddaughter needed was to be heard, to have her emotions recognized, and to be "mirrored."

So often, when we do Inner Child work, we try to tell our Inner Child, who went through trauma years ago, that it wasn't so bad, that it's alright now, that there's nothing to worry about. The fact is, it *was* so bad for the child at that time, and by saying it wasn't we are diminishing and even obliterating the Inner Child's experience. If the Inner Child is to remain sane and intact, it has no choice but to continue to fight back internally, trying to prove to us how terrible the situation actually was. The Inner Child does not need to be fixed. It needs to be heard and felt. And so do adults who are upset and in trouble. Making it better is not always doing something. It's often just listening and being with the other person.

🍂 We Can Be Kind to Ourselves 🍂

When you are feeling anxious or angry to a degree that doesn't seem appropriate to what's going on in the present, it is often because an upset that happened to your Inner Child a long time ago is being restimulated by your present circumstances. This is not a bad thing. In fact, it's a chance to heal, to hear and acknowledge the previously unheard, unacknowledged Inner Child who wasn't heard or seen at the time of the original incident. The way to contact this Inner Child is to sit quietly, feel whatever physical sensations you're having, and simply sit with them and experience them, even if (in fact especially if) they are uncomfortable. In this way, you give your Inner Child a chance to show you what he or she experienced, and you begin to heal and integrate old wounds.

🍂 We Can Be Kind in the World 🍂

1. Go to the Post Office at Christmas, pick up a letter that a child sent to Santa Claus, and anonymously fulfill the child's every request.

2. When you see someone homeless on the street, stop for a moment to speak with them, or at least meet their eye and say hello. Although money is what they seem to want, human kindness is usually what they're lacking the most. Make it better by providing it in some form, either with money, food, or conversation.

3. Give to charity. Volunteer. See where your money or your time, given kindly can make a difference in someone else's life.

CHAPTER 6

How Do We Make It Through?

This is another question we often ask ourselves when we encounter a situation we don't know how we're going to handle. How are we going to survive it? How are we going to navigate it without "losing it?!" How do we get to the other side? There's an expression: "When you're walking through hell, keep walking." This is often extremely challenging to do. When we hit seemingly impossible situations, we must ask ourselves, "What else can I do to help myself, or someone else, make it through?"

One Moment at a Time

In healing and twelve-step programs, we often hear the phrase "One Day at a Time." The idea is that when we have a problem that seems overwhelming, we can't think about the whole thing at once, but rather just deal with it on this day.

Years ago I was visiting a friend who was dying of AIDS. He was in that stage where he was experiencing many painful and uncomfortable diseases at the same time. Even with this, he seemed present, was glad to see me, and was able to experience the love and support that was being given to him by so many friends and family members. When I asked him how he did it, he said, "I've found that 'One Day at a Time' is much too long a time period to bite off when I'm in this condition. I am learning to take things 'One Second at a Time.' In this tiny time period, I can handle what's happening to me right now without worrying about the future. This gives me the room to experience everything that's going on in this second, which includes a lot of love, a lot of possibility, and a lot of relationship."

☁ We Can Be Kind to Ourselves ☁

My grandmother-in-law, who was a wise and successful older woman, used to say, "Live for today and let tomorrow take care of itself." When you find yourself in a circumstance where you are worried about the future or are feeling overwhelmed or hopeless, practice being in this second only. Just be here, let your mind focus on what you're experiencing physically, on what's around you, on who is with you, and on what you're doing right now. You'll find that by taking things one moment at a time you can make it through. This practice of breaking up a large problem into tiny, manageable chunks of time is being Kind to yourself.

🍫 We Can Be Kind in the World 🍫

1. When you see someone who is struggling with something, if you have something that would help them, whether it's money, time spent with them, or the ability to do errands for them, give it to them. No questions asked, no strings attached, even anonymously if that seems to be the only way they would take it.

2. When someone asks you for directions to a place that's nearby, take them there personally.

3. When you see someone who looks lost or upset, go up to them and ask them if they need help.

CHAPTER 7

What Can We Do When There's Nothing We Can Do?

Sometimes there is nothing we can do to change a circumstance or get rid of a problem. Someone close to us, or we ourselves, have a terminal illness. It's not going to get better. We've missed the plane and we are going to be late. There's no way around it. Our candidate has lost the election and that's that. We got fired from our job and there's no way we're going to get it back. We're going to a party and our favorite outfit just doesn't fit and there's no way for us to get into it. Or we didn't get invited to a party we wanted to go to. We've been dumped and a relationship we thought was going to continue is irrevocably over. Or we hear about someone who's having success at something that we wanted to have success at, and we're feeling angry or jealous. Or our computer crashed and we lost information we needed and we can't get it back. The list goes on. What can we do when there's *nothing* we can do?

Not Good, Not Bad

This has always been one of my favorite Buddhist stories, as it represents the idea that we never know what anything is for and that we never know whether anything is ultimately good or bad, no matter how it seems at the moment. Everything that happens can turn out to lead us to something good if we don't judge it and just allow events to unfold.

Here's the story:

A poor farmer was destitute and felt he had no hope of improving his lot. Then one day, out of nowhere, a beautiful horse wandered onto his farm. The farmer thought to himself, "How wonderful that this horse came to me. I needed a horse to make my farm work better and now one has come to me. The fact that this horse showed up is a good thing!"

The wise Buddhist would say, "Maybe it's good. Maybe it's bad. Who knows?"

The next day, the farmer's son was riding the horse and he fell off and broke his leg. The farmer was distraught, thinking, "How terrible that this horse showed up so that my son should break his leg. If this horse hadn't shown up, this never would have happened. This is a bad thing that this horse showed up and because of him my son broke his leg."

The wise Buddhist would say, "Maybe it's good. Maybe it's bad. Who knows?"

The next day, the army conscription officer showed up and drafted all the young men in the village. But since the farmer's son had a broken leg, the officer did not draft him and he was able to stay home, heal, and help on the farm. Seeing this, the farmer thought, "How wonderful that that horse showed up so my son could break his leg and not be drafted into the army."

Again, the wise Buddhist would say, "Maybe it's good. Maybe it's bad. Who knows?"

Can you see that this sequence goes on forever? There is always a next event and we never know whether we will call it good or bad. But whatever happens, the event will always lead to another event. So if we are being kind to ourselves, rather than stopping and worrying about a particular event, we can always know that it is possible that it will lead to something that we will call good. In this context, we can call everything good. Calling everything good is being kind to ourselves, because it puts us in a state where we worry less and have more hope, joy, and serenity.

A Broken Dish is an Opportunity for Kindness

Early in our relationship, my partner Shawn could at times be (how shall I put it?)…prickly! Loud noises and surprises tended to startle him, and he would often react with anger or upset. Added to this, he would sometimes then "awfulize," going down the path of how not only was this event terrible but how it would lead to terrible things in the future. It was the way in which he released his anxiety. Unfortunately, he often released it onto me!

One time, about an hour before we were expecting guests for a dinner party, I opened the refrigerator and a vegetable casserole fell out and smashed into smithereens on the floor. Shawn was standing right there and, knowing how he often reacted to such things, I found myself bracing for the worst. To my shock, Shawn looked at me and said, "That's OK. These things happen." He then looked over his shoulder and mockingly said, "Who said that?" referring to the fact that it was quite out of character for him to be so forgiving in an upsetting situation like this, where there was nothing that could be done about it. I can't tell you how relieved I felt that he reacted in this way. The next thing he said was, "You go upstairs and take your shower and I'll clean it up." I have never forgotten that moment of Kindness.

It was extremely gratifying to see how a potentially upsetting situation like this, where something had been broken and a dish we had planned to serve could not be salvaged, became instead an opportunity for a moment of kindness and the sharing of love and understanding. This incident created a big shift in our thinking and in our relationship, and more and more we began to use incidents like this as an opportunity to remember that when all else fails, We Can Be Kind.

🍂 We Can Be Kind to Ourselves 🍂

The next time an event occurs which you automatically think of as bad, stop and say to yourself, "I do not know what this is for." See if you can hold the idea that good can come out of it in ways you can't imagine. You don't have to figure it out, you just have to hold the thought. In this way you allow the possibility that everything can be for the good to infuse your thoughts. And when you do this, you begin to look for the good, you begin to notice the good in places you might not have noticed it before, and you begin to allow in good things that your former attitude might not have allowed. This is being kind to yourself.

🍂 We Can Be Kind in the World 🍂

1. When a friend, relative, or simply someone you encounter is in a situation where there is nothing you can do to change it, like an illness, death of someone close to them, or a loss of some other kind, try simply being there with them, not trying to fix or help them but simply being present.

2. When someone asks you for help that you cannot give, be truthful with them and tell them straight out, "I can't do that." When you have something that is difficult to say, like you have to break up with someone or fire someone or disappoint them in some way, the kind thing to do is often to simply tell them directly. I have found that people often truly appreciate being told something difficult honestly. It may be difficult for them to deal with, but when they know what they're up against, there are forces and powers within them that they can access to get themselves through whatever challenges the situation has presented to them. Often, in fact, these very losses lead to more self-realization, more power, and positive outcomes that would not have been possible had you not told them the truth.

3. The next time something that jangles your nerves or raises your hackles happens, whether it be something breaking or someone cutting you off on the road, notice the sensations you're having, notice the thoughts you're having, and then consciously decide to be kind. Smile at the other driver, tell the person who broke something that it's perfectly OK, or pick up the cat who just knocked over the vase and tell him that that must have been scary and that you love him. Try it. Rather

than escalating the upset with your own expression of upset, notice your upset but choose to be kind, and watch how that kindness adds love and joy and relief to the situation for all parties concerned.

CHAPTER 8

We Can Be Kind

When I wrote this line, I realized that the main word in it is actually "Can." Kindness is a choice that we can make no matter what is happening, no matter how helpless we feel, no matter how hopeless the situation seems. Kindness is something that is *always* available to us. It doesn't have to change anything. It is not limited by *any* circumstance (although we often find it hard to find kindness within ourselves when something really upsets us). No matter how difficult kindness can be to find at times, it is *always* there, within us. It is *always* a possibility. This possibility *never* goes away. It *never* becomes unavailable. And what does kindness do? What does your kind remark of understanding do when the person behind the counter at the airline has had to tell a hundred and fifty people that their flight is cancelled and is now telling you? What does kindness on your part do when you're trying to renegotiate your mortgage and the bank officer is telling you they can't do it? What does kindness do when someone cuts in front of you on the highway? What does kindness do when a little kid is behaving annoyingly in public? What does kindness do when you see a performance that you don't think was up to par and you have to go backstage and talk to the performer? What does kindness do when someone is being unkind to you?

Negotiating Rule #1—Be Kind

A number of years ago, I found myself in financial difficulty. We had bought a new house and were doing a tremendous amount of renovation. In order to pay for it, I took out a $362,000 second mortgage at 8 ¼ percent! (An exorbitant rate, I know, but that's what such loans were going for at that time.) I paid for the renovations (which resulted in our home being absolutely gorgeous) and invested the rest in the stock market, which was flying high at the time.

All of a sudden the stock market crashed, and meeting my monthly bills became a challenge. I immediately refinanced my first mortgage at a lower rate, but when I tried to refinance my second mortgage (which was the real money drain since it was at 8¼ percent), the bank put me through three months of asking for paper after paper, chart after chart, figure after figure…and then turned me down. As time went on and I watched interest rates dropping precipitously, I became more and more upset. I went through the refinancing process five times, each time spending months sending the bank the same figures over and over again, each time being turned down in the end. And boy was I angry, screaming at people over the phone, threatening, calling them and the bank they worked for names—you name it, I said it.

After five failed attempts to modify my loan, I was at my wits end. So I picked up the phone, called the bank, and said, "I get it. You're waiting for me to run out of money before you'll do anything." To which they said, "Of course we're not doing that." To which I said, "Oh yes you are, and guess what. I just ran out of money!" And I stopped paying my loan.

What followed was a strange combination of one bank department not knowing what the other was doing. In the same day, I would get one letter saying "We're here to help" and another letter threatening to take my house away (which I knew they couldn't do, since my first mortgage was being paid.) They also completely destroyed my credit rating, to the point where when I was ready to lease my next car, my brother had to cosign for me.

I had a second home, which I realized I would have to sell. The sale might bring me enough money to partially pay off the loan, but if I continued to make payments at this rate, I would be in the same trouble within a couple of years. So I hired a lawyer for three thousand dollars because he said he could negotiate a settlement for between twenty-five and fifty cents on the dollar with the bank. He did nothing, telling me he had called and that the bank was not negotiating settlements at this time.

At my wits' end, I called up a friend who was a music industry dealmaker and worked a lot with banks. She offered to call the president of the bank and find out exactly who I needed to talk to in order to negotiate a settlement. She got me a name, sat me down, and gave me a piece of advice which changed everything. She told me: "No matter what, no matter what they say, no matter how they threaten, no matter how scared you are, *always* be delightful, charming, upbeat, and pleasant." In other words, always be kind. She reminded me that the people I was dealing with were not the bank, but regular people who were employees; they were just doing their job, and I could get much further by not insulting them or intimidating them. I put a note-to-self next to the phone. *Always* be kind.

I contacted the person to whom I'd been referred at the bank's loan settlement department and she asked me to send her the same pile of papers, facts, and lists that I'd been asked to send five times before. Since I was now not making the payments, I was in no rush, so I pleasantly filled them out and sent them off. Three months in a row, I got the same request for the same facts and I simply sent them off.

One day, I got a call from her saying, "We need a settlement statement." I asked, "What's a settlement statement?" She said that since I wanted to settle the loan for less, I had to make them an offer. I very pleasantly said that I had no money. She responded that I had to offer them something. I said that I could probably scrape together $5,000. She answered, "Mr. Friedman, are you aware that this is a $362,000 loan?" I laughed pleasantly and said, "Dear, I am aware of *that* every day." We both laughed. There was no contention; we were just discussing something pleasantly.

She then said, "We couldn't possibly take a number that low. We would have to have at least $123,000. Well that was interesting. My $362,000 loan had suddenly been cut down to $123,000. I told her I would see what I could do and get back to her.

I called my brother and he agreed to give me $20,000 if that would take care of the loan. I then had some jewelry appraised that my mother had left when she passed, and discovered that I could get $6,250 for it. So I called the lady from the bank back and told her that I'd been able to come up with $31,250 if that would clear the loan. Her response was, "That's not even 10%." I asked, "Would you take 10% if I could get it?" to which she said, "No, we would need at least $90,000." We were now at $90,000. I pleasantly told her I didn't have that, but would investigate and see what I could do.

The following week I got a surprise royalty check in the mail, so I called her back and said, "I got a surprise check in the mail so I could give you $36,200 (which was 10%). She said that that was still way too low, and that they would need at least $68,000. We were now at $68,000 on a loan that had originally been $362,000.

I told her I didn't know how I could get that much and asked her what would happen next. She said that I had ninety days to accept the offer. If I accepted it, great. If I didn't, the whole mortgage would go into collections. I told her I would do my best, thanked her for her help, and hung up.

A month later my second property sold and left me with a little more money. I called her back and asked if she might possibly accept $50,000. She said, "No, we would need at least $54,000." I said, "Deal!" So I ended up paying off a $362,000 loan for $54,000. Fourteen cents on the dollar. The whole transaction had been civil, in fact pleasant, and I felt very kindly toward this woman. In fact, I felt very kindly toward the bank, where I had "hated" them and been "furious" before, and could really appreciate that they had ultimately been willing to work with me and that they had made this compromise available to me.

I was kind, they were kind, and we got an outcome that allowed me to avoid bankruptcy and enabled them to get something back on their loan. Since that time, I always try to remember to be kind during negotiations, no matter how upsetting what's coming from the other side of the phone seems to be.

🍂 We Can Be Kind to Ourselves 🍂

Don't "awfulize." The next time something upsetting happens, don't project into the future. When you're late for something, don't say to yourself (or to someone who's with you), "Now we'll never find a parking spot and then we'll be late and we'll miss the show and we won't be able to find a place to eat and all will be lost." The reason we awfulize is often because we're not able to stay with the uncomfortable sensations that arise when something goes "wrong." Instead of going into your mind, go into your body and simply feel where you feel uncomfortable. Stay with that discomfort and know that no incident is hopeless, unlimited possibilities always exist, and you're going to be OK no matter what happens. This is being kind to ourselves, and it leaves us open to unthought-of possibilities inherent in any situation, even one that seems troubling or hopeless.

🍂 We Can Be Kind in the World 🍂

1. The next time you get into a difficult or upsetting negotiation, whether it's an airline that's cancelled your

flight, a service person who won't give you satisfaction, or someone who treats you rudely, try being pleasant and kind. It doesn't mean you don't ask for what you want or aren't firm. You just do it kindly. There's a wonderful expression that Al-Anon groups often use: "Say what you mean, mean what you say, don't say it mean." Kindness pays off not only in results, but in how the whole transaction feels and in the love, communication, and human relatedness that can be shared, even in contentious circumstances.

2. Do not fight unkindness with unkindness. Do not fight attack with attack. This not only empowers the unkindness and the attack but also keeps it going. This is sometimes often very difficult to do when we feel provoked, but if we don't do this, we become the very thing we say we are fighting against. Mother Theresa said, "I would never go to an anti-war rally, because by definition an anti-war rally requires that there be a war to fight against. I would definitely go to a pro-peace rally." State what you are for, not what you're against. This is the best way to reduce resistance and promote understanding and, as such, is the kind thing to do.

3. Kindness comes in all sorts of forms. Sometimes kindness is being nice: holding a door, telling someone they look nice, giving someone a gift, being polite. Sometimes kindness is being tough: refusing to enable an addict, telling an overly dependent child they're on their own, not bailing someone out financially when they need to learn how to do it themselves. Sometimes kindness is telling the truth (when someone's hearing the truth would help them or the situation). Sometimes kindness is not telling the truth (when the truth would only hurt someone and not do any good). In every circumstance, before you act, think to yourself, "What would be the kindest thing I could do at this moment?" and do that. As the song says, "We *can* be kind." We always have that choice.

CHAPTER 9

We Can Take Care of Each Other

Even in the "worst" of circumstances, we have the ability to experience a sense of serenity and power when we take the focus off of ourselves and our problems and take care of someone else. Often things we can't do for ourselves we can do for others. I have a lot of trouble making certain phone calls on my own behalf, whereas I can easily make them for a friend. So taking care of somebody else reminds me of my own power.

Panic Attack

Years ago, my father was having a panic attack on a crowded, hot subway car and was terrified that he was going to faint. All of a sudden, as they pulled into a station, the woman next to him actually did faint. My father immediately picked her up, carried her onto the platform, and stayed with her until she revived. All his thoughts of fainting were gone, since he had put his attention on someone else.

Heaven or Hell

There's a wonderful set of lithographs that I saw once that expresses this point perfectly. The first is called "Hell." It depicts a large, round table filled with food, and around it are sitting people whose arms are much longer below the elbow than above it. Because of this, none of them are able to feed themselves, because they can't get the food to their mouths. The second lithograph depicts the same table and the same people with the same deformed arms, but they are reaching across the table, feeding each other. That one is called "Heaven." When it seems that nothing can be done, we can still always take care of each other.

©Stuart McMillen

Kamikaze Drive-by Prayer

My friend Mitchell Savage used to practice something which he called "Kamikaze Drive-by Prayer." In the morning, he would think of someone who he felt could use his support. He would think of what they might need and spend a few moments praying for them. Throughout the day, whenever he thought of it, he would send prayers their way. Then at the end of the day he would give them a call and ask them how their day went. Invariably, something wonderful had happened for them—sometimes big things, sometimes just a sense of comfort and safety. It made Mitchell feel wonderful too.

Secret Santa

Every year, the US Post Office receives thousands of letters from children simply addressed to "Santa Claus, North Pole." They keep these letters at the Post Office, and people can go in, take one or more, and anonymously fulfill the requests that the children have made.

The year after the 9/11 attack in New York City, I decided to do this. So I went to the Post Office and picked up a letter from a third grader. The letter read something like this:

Dear Santa,

I don't know if you even exist, but if you do, I'd like to ask you for a few things. My daddy lost his job and my mommy doesn't work, so we don't have any money for presents this year. I know I'm lucky to have a mommy and daddy, and I feel terrible for those children who lost parents in the World Trade Center.

If you could, I would like some chapter books, a bear, and some things for my computer. Thank you Santa, and have a Merry Christmas.

When I saw this letter, something in me said, "I'm going to go all out."

First I went to Barnes & Noble and asked the clerk what chapter books were. As one might expect, they were books with chapters, and apparently this was a very important milestone for third graders—to finally read a book that had chapters instead of "baby books." So I picked up a bunch of chapter books.

Then I went to Toys R Us and bought the biggest bear I could find. It was bigger than me. It was expensive, but so what.

Then I went to Kmart and bought a four hundred dollar gift certificate.

I took some red stationery and wrote:

Santa Claus

North Pole

Dear _____

I received your letter, and I was so impressed with it that I'm sending you this package. I've put in some chapter books I thought you might like, and I hope you like the bear I picked out for you. I know you wanted some computer things, so to make sure you could get exactly what you need, I bought this gift certificate. Have your mommy and daddy take you to Kmart where you can pick out exactly what you want.

Have a Merry Christmas, and never forget: "Dreams can come true!"

Love,
Santa

I went down to Mail Boxes Etc., where they wrapped this *huge* package, and since it was an answer to a letter from Santa, they charged me half-price to ship it. This child will never know who sent it, but I got such pleasure out of thinking about her receiving it.

As I left the Post Office, I couldn't help but notice that I felt fantastic. As I thought about it, the feelings I felt had nothing to do with the idea that I had been so generous. Rather, I realized that I was now certain that I live in a world where dreams can be fulfilled by someone I've never met in ways I couldn't imagine. How did I know that? Because I had just done that for someone else, and by doing that, I had now proven that this is possible. For someone else. And for *me.* I had created a better, safer, more compassionate, and kinder world for myself because I had given to someone else. I had taken care of someone, so who knew when and where someone might take care of me.

If You Can Do Something for Someone Else, Do It

Years ago I had brought my friend Kathie Lee Gifford to my friend Dave Wilde's basement recording studio to record an album. The studio was in the basement of Dave's parents' home in New Jersey. At one point, Dave's mother, who usually walked around in a housecoat during the day, came down to say hello. She was dressed to the nines, hair done, full makeup. Obviously she had dressed up because she knew she was going to meet one of her favorite television stars. Kathie Lee was very gracious and stopped the session to chat. At one point, Dave's mother tentatively said, "My best girlfriend is upstairs. Might it be possible for her to meet you?" Kathie turned to Dave and asked, "Are we in a hurry?" to which Dave replied, "No, we have plenty of time." Then she turned to Dave's mother and said, "Do you have some tea?" Kathie then proceeded to go upstairs with Dave's mother and spent a half hour having "tea with the girls." It was the thrill of a lifetime for these two suburban women to be sitting down chatting with their favorite morning TV host.

Later, when I mentioned to Kathie how kind that was, she said, "You know, I know I'm no great shakes, and that I'm no better than anyone else, but if it's going to make someone's day to have a conversation with me or have me sign my name to a program or piece of paper, why not do it?" I never forgot that, and over the years, I've seen how not only is it no skin off my back to be kind to someone, but in truth, it makes *my* day!

Wishing Someone You "Can't Stand" Well

When my ex left me suddenly many years ago, I *hated* him! I could not, in any way, wish him well. As time went on, and I really looked at this, I began to realize that the main reason I was holding on to my resentment was because I thought that I, myself, could not be happy. On an unconscious level, his happiness was reflecting my own unhappiness back to me. I slowly began to understand that if I were truly happy, and had love and success and everything I wanted in my life, I would have no reason to wish him unhappiness.

At this point, rather than focusing on him (which meant I was actually focusing on my own shortcomings), I began to focus on the infinite possibilities of love and success that existed for me. Within a few years, I was doing what I really wanted to do, living where I really wanted to live, and in love with someone I really wanted to be in love with. As I look back on it today, my resentment has turned to gratitude that things happened exactly as they did, because had they not, I would not have all the joy, contentment, and abundance that his leaving me allowed me to find. And with this gratitude, I'm also fine with his being happy and healthy and finding whatever it is he truly desires.

This form of forgiveness does not mean that you have to like someone or like what they've done. A few years after my breakup, the man with whom my ex had had the blatant affair that ultimately caused him to leave sent me an email asking if he might speak to me. I asked him, "About what?" and he wrote, "About an abject apology." I was fascinated to notice that my response was, "If you feel you need to apologize to me, you're welcome to, but I have to tell you, I've long ago forgiven you. In fact, I'm extremely grateful to you, because if you had not come into the picture and done what you'd done, I might have never been released to find the happy life I'm living today." His response was: "I knew you'd say that, but I feel so guilty about the role I played." To which I said, "Listen, that's not for me to absolve you of. I don't like you, I don't like what you did, and I have no desire to be friends with you. But I do forgive you and thank you. It's up to you to handle your part inside yourself." I never heard from him again. And interestingly enough, I do hope he found a way to find inner peace, and perhaps learned something and might change his future behavior.

Being Happy For Someone Else's Success

At times, I've found myself being resentful of someone who has success in an area in which I wish I was having success. I'll notice that I'm hoping a particular Broadway show, movie, or even a relationship fails. As is the case with being unable to wish an "ex" well, this can only be because I feel that I can't have the success that I'm seeing someone else has. Only when I can be happy for someone else having success can I open up the possibilities and make real moves toward my own success in the same area. So although wishing someone else success is, of course, being kind to the other person, it's just as much about being kind to ourselves. I often measure my own success and sense of happiness and well-being by how happy and excited I can be for someone else's success in the same area.

🐾 We Can Be Kind to Ourselves 🐾

When we fly, we are always told that in the case of a loss of pressure in the cabin, we should put on our own oxygen mask before helping someone next to us, even if that person is a child or a helpless older person. The same applies to kindness. In order to be truly kind to others, we must be able to be kind to ourselves. So while you're taking care of others, always make sure you're taking care of yourself. Eat right, get enough sleep, do things you enjoy, work on things you want to work on. Doing this will keep your reservoir of kindness available and will prevent you from becoming depleted or resentful.

🌰 We Can Be Kind in the World 🌰

1. When you're doing a job for someone, let your words and actions show that you care as much about getting it right as they do. When someone is having a problem you're helping them with, let your words and actions show that you are treating it as though it were your problem. When you are staying in someone's home, treat their possessions as carefully as you would if they were your possessions, and earn your keep with kindness by making their life as easy as possible. Make the bed, help with the dishes, clean up after yourself.

2. When you are applying for a job, rather than thinking of it as "I need a job and I hope they give it to me," come into the interview with the attitude of "What can I do for you?" Make it clear to your prospective employer that you are here to help him or her, here to make his or her life easier, and here to help your employer reach his or her goals. My most successful interviews were when I took the lead in asking my prospective employers what they needed and then showed them that I could deliver it.

3. "Taking care of each other" is a very important part of partnership and marriage. If your partner has a need or a fragility that you might think is ridiculous, understand that they need care in that area and take care of them rather than criticizing. My partner has an inordinate fear of mice. Although I think it's ridiculous, I close the door to the house the second I come inside so mice won't follow me in, I walk down the center of the street in New York with him to avoid running into a mouse that might be coming out of the garbage, and when he thinks there may be a dead mouse lying on the kitchen floor and can't go into the room, I go in, turn on the lights, and pick up the chunk of dryer lint on the floor that, in the dimness, looked to him like it might have been a mouse. And I do it without comment and without judgment. This is taking care of him, and taking care of him is more important to me than being right or changing him. See where your partner or spouse or friend has a fragility that you can take care of rather than judge. This is kindness.

4. When you are in a position where you can do something for someone else, do it! Even if it might be inconvenient for you, even if you're getting something for someone else that you have not been able to get for yourself,

do it. If you can make a contact for someone, make it. If you can offer someone words of encouragement, offer them. If you can teach someone something they need to know, teach it. If someone needs something from you that you can provide, provide it, even if it's a little uncomfortable or takes up your time. And pause to notice how *you* feel when you perform any one of these kindnesses for someone else.

CHAPTER 10

We Can Remember That Deep Down Inside We All Need The Same Thing

This is the thing we so often forget when we encounter conflict. We are all the same inside. We all want the same things: love, encouragement, attention, peace, success. It's a tenet of acting that when you play a villain, you can't play him as though he were evil. You are living inside this person, so you have to connect with his deepest desires, why he feels he has to act this way, what he needs and wants. When we look at other people, especially when they disagree with us or seem to be in our way, it can be hard to remember that they are just like us inside—human—and want the same thing. The person behind the counter at the airport, whom we regard as not giving us what we want because the plane was cancelled, may feel terrible to be disappointing all of these people, even though it's not her fault, and may be very anxious about being yelled at by angry customers. I know of countless examples of flights being cancelled, where one person comes up (sometimes that one person has been me) and takes the time to consider how difficult it is for the employee having to deal with all these disgruntled people. More often than not, if anyone gets another flight out quickly or gets bumped to First Class, it's the one who has been kind.

Election Politics

The year 2016 saw what was certainly one of the most contentious and divided elections in American history. With social media so readily available to so many, the attacks, the anger, and each side's dismissal of the other's point of view were rampant. In most cases, each side was simply preaching to the choir, since nobody seemed to be willing to listen to the other side's point of view.

In an unusual show of willingness to listen, one friend of mine, a well-known songwriter who has spent much of her life in deep spiritual pursuits, put up a post that essentially said the following:

"I would like to hear from anyone who is supporting (name of other candidate) why they are supporting him, what they think he will do for them, and what they think is positive about him. I respectfully request that when these posts go up, there be no rebuttals, no attacks, no opinions from the other side. I simply want to hear from the people who are voting for this candidate so I can understand why they are doing this."

When we really stop and listen to the "other side," what we discover is that although we may seem to want totally different things, a different candidate, different ways of running the government, a different tone of voice, different laws, etc., underneath we all do truly want the same things: to be safe, to be happy, to have a livelihood, and to have love in our lives. Only when we know this can we begin to see that our "enemies" are truly like us deep down inside, and begin to work from this commonality to come to solutions that are good for us all.

Uniting for a Common Cause

It's interesting how we've arbitrarily divided the world into countries, religions, races, colors, sexual orientations, ideologies, etc. that emphasize our differences rather than what we have in common: the fact that we are all members of the human race. I've often thought that the thing that would bring all the countries of the world together and have them share their power, their commitment, their forces, and their technology would be if Mars attacked us. We would suddenly have a common enemy, think of ourselves as one united planet, and work for a common cause. I wonder if we might do this without having to have Mars attack us.

The Truth About Christmas

Years ago, I was asked to write a Christmas song for a benefit concert. As I thought about Christmas, all the annoying things about the holiday came to mind: the weather, the traffic, the obligations, the cards, the Santa Claus myth, the family dynamics, etc. As I wrote about all these, I wondered how I was going to bring the song around so that it would have a message that would be of value. In working on it, I ultimately came to a true understanding of what our commonality is and why we go through all the "hassles" of the holiday every year.

Here's the lyric:

"The Truth About Christmas"
Words & Music by David Friedman

Christmas Time is almost here
Presents under the tree
Christmas comes but once a year
And that's enough for me

Here's the Truth about Christmas
There is no Santa Claus
No reindeer fly him in
No one's rewarding you
According to how good or bad you have been
It just seems too unfair
Sometimes it's hard to bear
the Truth about Christmas

Here's the Truth about Christmas
I'm always low on cash
when it comes time to shop

And on the day I go
There's always snow and sleet and hail
that won't stop
And sending cards, required
Well I'm just sick and tired
That's the Truth about Christmas

And then I take the plane
It's always late and crowded
Two buses and a train might be faster
though I doubt it
'Cause everybody in the world
Has the same idea as me
They think they'll find the milk of human kindness
in the bosom of their family

Here's the Truth about Christmas
It's hardly ever fun
'Cause families always fight
Though things start out alright
Before the night has barely even begun

They've had too much to drink
And told you what they think
That's the Truth about Christmas

So why do I still care?
Why do I still do it?
Why do I keep going there
and keep on struggling through it?
Why does hope leap in my heart
when the Christmas carols start?
And why do I still feel a glow on Christmas
even knowing what I know?

Here's the Truth about Christmas
I want it to be nice
I want it to be fun
And as I've looked around
what I have found is
so does everyone
So Christmas makes me see
That everyone's like me
The pain I'm going through
Is pain that they're all feeling too
And it's so encouraging
to know we all want the same thing

To be loved
To be happy
To have hope
That's the Truth about Christmas
Hope!

❧ We Can Be Kind to Ourselves ❧

The next time you find yourself in a circumstance where you feel obligation or annoyance or a sense of contention, look at all the other people around you who are in the same circumstance and see if you can find the common ground among you. When you can have the awareness that everyone around you is, in some way or another, having the same struggles, you can empathize and feel connected to everyone else. By doing this, by internally experiencing a sense of being kind to others in this way, you are also being kind to yourself in that you begin to feel less left out, less different, less alone, and more a part of things.

🕸 We Can Be Kind in the World 🕸

1. The next time you have a disagreement with someone, put yourself in their shoes. Ask yourself, if you were them, in their situation, what you would want. Then, seeing them as yourself, treat them with the respect and courtesy with which you would hope to be treated. Another way of saying this is, when you think you lack something or are not getting something from the world or from someone else, *give* that very thing to someone else. If you notice that people aren't getting back to you when you email them, make sure you're getting back to everyone who emails you. In that way, *you* create the world *you* want to live in.

2. The next time you find yourself in an altercation or disagreement, try stopping and asking the other person to explain what they want and why they want it. See if, instead of arguing, you can simply hear it. And then, do everything you can to deal positively with what they want rather than fighting it. That is being kind, and ultimately kindness begets kindness. Strangely enough, it is the best way to get your own needs fulfilled, even when they conflict with what the other person wants.

3. In dealing with people from different cultures, different religions and different sexual persuasions, see if you can view them simply as human beings like yourself and can see that deep down inside they want the exact same things as you: peace, respect, happiness, safety. Look past the differences and offer them the kindness that you would want to be offered. Seeing them as the same as you, and treating them as such, creates a bond of cooperation and mutuality rather than conflict. The best way to get what you want and need is to see that underneath our surface differences, we are all the same. When we know this, we know that everyone has the capacity to understand everyone else's needs because everyone has the same basic needs.

CHAPTER 11

---

*And Maybe We'll Find, If We
Are There For Each Other,
That Together We'll Weather
Whatever Tomorrow May Bring*

When we have challenges and problems, especially ones that seem unsolvable, they offer us an opportunity to connect to other people, to get out of ourselves, and to realize that if we enlist other people's support and lend our support to other people, we can get through things we thought we couldn't get through. Being "there" for each other means seeing and accepting people as they are, having empathy for others as well as opening ourselves up to help. Over the years I've come to understand that for me, the definition of love is simply to see without judgment, without trying to fix someone else, without thinking that anything is "wrong" with someone else, no matter how different their problems or their understanding may be from our own. It's only when we can "love" in this way that we can really be *there* for each other. When we do this, we get a deeper understanding of life that lets us know that it's not about achievement or success or failure or money or anything physical, but about the fact that we're all in this together. If we all realized this, so many conflicts we experience would not happen, and we could truly weather, as connected beings, whatever comes our way.

Funerals, Terminal Illnesses, and Hopeless Situations

For many years I wrote music for the annual Duke Children's Hospital Benefit. Every spring I would spend a few days in Durham, North Carolina, rehearsing and putting on a show. In my spare time, I would always make it a point to visit the kids who were in the Children's Hospital. I found it especially moving to visit children who were undergoing stem cell replacement. What this meant was that they had to be totally isolated for several weeks, and anyone who came to visit them had to completely suit up in germ-proof suits. Their parents, especially the mothers, would spend those weeks just sitting in the isolation rooms with their children, who were struggling with leukemia and other kinds of cancers. You would think that this would be depressing, but for some strange reason I always found these visits soothing, comforting, and, in a strange way, joyful. As I thought about why, I realized that the reason there was such a sense of peace about this place was that everyone here was remembering something that most of us forget. They were not thinking about their careers or whether they could make more money or impress the neighbors. They were not thinking about petty difficulties and small aggravations. They were acutely aware that the only thing that is important is Love. These places were filled with Love, with caring, and with people working together to be with each other and do the best they could, even when the outcome of the situation seemed hopeless.

Have you ever noticed that funerals, no matter how sad, also can have this quality? Everyone gets together to express their love for the person who is gone, and for each other. Focus on work and on the business of everyday living is suspended, people take off from their jobs, people are just together. So a funeral, as upsetting as it may be, is another opportunity for love and kindness, perhaps for seeing people you haven't seen in a long while and reconnecting.

Events like 9/11 and the AIDS crisis, as tragic as they were and are, transformed people because they came together. I was in New York when 9/11 happened. In fact, I watched the buildings go down. It was truly horrifying, but the coming together of New Yorkers, people who normally ignored each other suddenly smiling and talking to each other on the subway, people coming to each others' aid, was truly inspiring. Not that we ever hope events like this will happen, but if we can use then to bring out human kindness then they are not totally in vain. The start of the AIDS crisis was one of the most terrifying and helplessness-creating events of our generation. People were getting sick, there was nothing that could be done about it, and the pain, panic, and frustration were enormous. But something that began to happen was that people began to band together to support each other, to contribute hope and money and time and research, and communities became aware that even if they couldn't cure it, they could experience kindness and love and a sense of connection. It may have been a horrible price to pay, but through kindness, many, many people were able to find good where there seemed to be none.

Laughing with a Dying Friend

A number of years ago, I got a call telling me that a well-known writer I'd worked with in New York theater and in several movies was on his last legs in his battle with AIDS. I was told that if I wanted to see him alive, I had to come down right away. I came down and there he was in bed, this gifted, bright, good-looking young man, curled up in a fetal position, blind, weighing about sixty-five pounds. I moved close to his ear and said, "Hi, it's David. I'm here." He mumbled something and I said, "I'm so sorry. I can't understand what you're saying." To which he answered, in a big loud voice, "Well *excuuuse* me! I'm dying!" We all got a good laugh. He died shortly thereafter. There was nothing I could do except be there, but being there gave us a lovely moment of connection to remember and allowed him to have his sense of humor until the end.

The Gift of Trouble

One of my favorite projects that I ever got to compose the music for was a musical version of the beloved Alaskan children's book *King Island Christmas*, by Jean Rogers. It's a true story of how an entire island community banded together to solve a common problem.

In this song, with lyrics by Deborah Brevoort, a mother tells her young child about the hidden gifts that can be found inside of a troubling situation.

"The Gift of Trouble"
Words by Deborah Brevoort
Music by David Friedman

Trouble can be the wrapping
For a gift that's really great
When trouble comes, don't despair
Try to appreciate
The chance that trouble gives you
To discover something new
The chance to find and uncover
Powerful things that are hidden in you

When the Gift of Trouble
Is put under your tree
Make yourself unwrap it
Take a deep breath

Pick up the box
Set it on your knee

Sometimes the bow is tied in a knot
The tape's too sticky
Your fingers get caught
You may not like the way the ribbon is tied
But open the box
There's a beautiful gift inside

Trouble is worth the trouble
Though it doesn't feel so great
When trouble comes, change your plans
Try to appreciate
The chance that trouble gives you
To see the problem through
The chance to find and uncover
Powerful things that are hidden in you

When the Gift of Trouble
Is put under your tree
Don't forget to say "thank you"
For the blessing or two
That is waiting for you
In the gift you cannot see

Sometimes the bow is tied in a knot
The tape's too sticky
Your fingers get caught
You may not like the way the ribbon is tied
But open the box
There's a beautiful gift inside
You've got to believe
There's a beautiful gift inside

🐾 We Can Be Kind to Ourselves 🐾

The next time you find yourself in a situation that appears to be hopeless, where there seems to be no solution, try to become aware that you are not alone. Not only are there always other people (whether you know them or not) who have the same problem or at least understand what it's like to be going through what you're going through, there are also invisible parts of yourself and of the universe that are always there to give you help and support when you open yourself to them. This is called Faith. It could be Faith that there is something unconscious inside of you that knows how to handle the problem in ways you aren't consciously aware of. It could be Faith in a Higher Power, in the God of Your Understanding, in Nature, in the Universe, in the Goodness of all people. Sit down quietly and ask yourself, "What is my unique and particular Faith? What do I believe in? What is possible?" And remember, Faith is never lacking in any of us, it's just a question of where we're putting our Faith. Are you putting your Faith in something negative, in worrying, in believing that there can't be a good outcome? If so, see if you can direct your Faith to something that serves and supports you better. It's all here. It's just a matter of where you look.

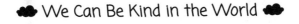 We Can Be Kind in the World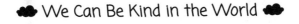

1. When someone you know is having a problem, try simply showing up. Bring a meal, bring a movie, bring a gift, or just simply bring yourself.

2. There is strength in numbers. If you have an issue that's troubling you, there must be others who are having that same issue. Join a support group. Go to a

march or rally. By doing this you are getting the help you need by being with like-minded people, but don't underestimate the help and support that your mere presence gives to other people.

3. Allow people to give things to you and accept them graciously. One of the kindest things you can do for someone is allowing them to experience their magnanimity, their power, and their ability to make a difference when you accept, with gratitude and open arms, a gift, a kindness, or even some kind of major help that you might feel is "too much." Get past any guilt or shame you might have about taking something and allow the other person to feel good about themselves because they have the power to give and make a difference for you.

WE CAN BE KIND: THE SOLUTION TO EVERY PROBLEM

"Three things in human life are important: the first is to be kind; the second is to be kind; and the third is to be kind."

—Henry James

"Guard well within yourself that treasure, kindness. Know how to give without hesitation, how to lose without regret, how to acquire without meanness."

—George Sand

"Kindness is in our power, even when fondness is not."

—Samuel Johnson

"The greatest work that kindness does to others is that it makes them kind themselves."

—Amelia Earhart

"Teach this triple truth to all: a generous heart, kind speech, and a life of service and compassion are the things which renew humanity."
—**Buddha**

"Wherever there is a human being, there is an opportunity for kindness."
—**Seneca**

"Always be kind, for everyone is fighting a hard battle."
—**Plato**

"Always be a little kinder than necessary."
—**James M. Barrie**

"There is no greater loan than a sympathetic ear."
—**Frank Tyger**

"Too often we underestimate the power of a touch, a smile, a kind word, a listening ear, an honest compliment, or the smallest act of caring, all of which have the potential to turn a life around."
—**Leo Buscaglia**

"Let Go and Let God."
—Unknown Origin

"Be nice."
—My Mother

CHAPTER 12

Nobody Really Wants to Fight, Nobody Really Wants to Go to War

When people hear this line, they often say, "Oh, that's not true. I know plenty of people who want to fight, who attack, who are aggressive and start conflicts. I know plenty of examples of countries being aggressive, invading other countries, and starting wars." The important word in this line is *really*. Although people may appear to want to fight and to start wars, deep down it's always because they are frustrated, they want something they can't get, or they are experiencing fear or anger that they either can't tolerate and contain or that has gone unseen by another human being. It can be very challenging, when we encounter an aggressor or an "enemy," to look past the surface and see the person and what they really need. For example, it's an axiom of the Al-Anon twelve-step program that when the alcoholic is attacking you, whatever they're saying to you is really what they're thinking about themselves. When you understand this, you don't attack back, because that would just make them feel worse and they would attack more. You learn to treat the alcoholic with love, respect, and understanding, no matter how they're behaving. In this way, you allow the tension and the opposition to unravel in its own time. So the next time you see someone who appears to "want" to fight, see if you can get past that and see what they are really asking for—what they really need.

Camp Common Bond

So often wars are started and maintained by countries for political or economic reasons, because one government feels that another government is thwarting them or opposed to them. What has always struck me is that, in most cases, the people of those countries have no gripe with each other; they often don't even think of each other except as other people like themselves. Countries may become enemies in the political sense, but the people in those countries don't have to be enemies.

During the height of the Israeli–Palestinian conflict, a camp was started in Pennsylvania called Camp Common Bond.

For several weeks, Palestinian and Israeli teenagers were flown to the US to go to camp together. These children had nothing against each other. They played together, they talked about their common problems, and they worked together. There was no sense whatsoever of their being enemies, nor even of their being different. They were all human, all teenagers. The concept proves that although leaders of countries may start wars, so often the people in those countries have no desire to be at war and hold no animosity toward the people of the other country. And often when people do hold animosity toward people of another country, it's because they've been told to by their governments, by propaganda, and by the news. These teenagers from supposedly opposing countries who spent a few weeks together not only often became lifelong friends, but were also able to bring a different point of view back to their families and friends in their own countries. They were able to begin to spread the point of view of love, tolerance, sameness, and Kindness.

Silent Night

In Stanley Weintraub's book *Silent Night*, he talks about an amazing incident that occurred on Christmas Eve on a battlefield in World War I. For days, the Germans had been battling against British and French troops on the fields of Flanders, each side dug into miles of trenches facing each other across the field. On Christmas Eve, small candlelit Christmas trees began to appear on the German side, and the Germans began to sing Christmas songs. Hearing this, the French and British troops began to respond with their own Christmas songs.

The German troops began to take the risk of climbing out of their trenches, holding up signs that read "If you don't fight, we won't fight." The French and British troops responded with signs saying "Merry Christmas." Gradually, the soldiers from both sides walked to the center and shook hands. Together, they buried the dead who lay on the battlefield and couldn't be reached because they were in the middle of the field. Then they exchanged gifts—supplies that they had, cake, alcohol, cigarettes—and in some places they even struck up games of soccer. The leaders of their governments may have hated each other and been at war, but these were young men, most in their early twenties, who, regardless of what side they were on or what country they were from, had a tremendous amount in common. They didn't want to fight. The politics of the day and the large movements of the world got them caught up in a war, but when left to their own devices they much preferred to be Kind.

🍂 We Can Be Kind to Ourselves 🍂

When you run into someone who is supposed to be "the enemy" either in your daily life or in business, see if you can look past the "idea" of who they're supposed to be and see that they are human just like you. Look into your heart and notice that you, deep down, have no desire to fight, and if they are just like you, they probably have no desire to fight either. Practice experiencing and having thoughts of Kindness in these situations and see what happens.

☁ We Can Be Kind in the World ☁

1. When someone wants to pick a fight with you, refuse to fight and see what happens. Usually people think they want to fight because they're afraid of being attacked or of losing something. Refuse to participate in that and see what happens.

2. When you are talking to a service person and they are being nasty to you, respond to them with kindness and see what happens. Often the person behind the counter, who is just a person like you, is feeling frustrated or afraid or is worried that they're going to be attacked, so they lash out. See them as not wanting to fight, treat them with kindness, and watch how the transaction turns out. I can't tell you how many times I've been bumped up to first class when my previous flight had been cancelled, had a loan officer give me a break on my mortgage when I'd been told there was no way the bank would do it, or gotten an upgrade to a suite in a hotel when there were "no rooms to be had" by simply being kind when the employee opposite me was starting to get tough or nasty. Try it.

3. In your relationships, when the other person starts to fight, listen to them and ask them what's troubling them rather than fighting with them. Usually people start fights because they feel they're not going to be heard. Let them know you hear them, treat them with kindness and respect, and see what happens.

CHAPTER 13

Everyone Wants to Make Things Right,
So What Are We Always Fighting For?

What if we looked at every action as people trying to make things right, to heal and fix problems? What if illness is the body's way of trying to heal? What if breakups, job losses, financial crises, or having a candidate you don't want in office get elected all have the possibility of "making things right"? What if things have to go downhill, or anger has to be expressed, or hidden prejudices or "negative" thoughts have to come to light in order for ultimate healing to take place? What if we were to view everyone as wanting to make things right, no matter how misguided they might seem to us? I know that in my collaborations as a theater writer, my collaborator is always trying to do the same thing as me. Make it right. Often he will have an idea that I think is ridiculous or stupid, but I always entertain it because I know that he is not only a talented writer, but he desperately wants to see whatever project we're working on be the best it can be. That doesn't mean we agree on what the best it can be is, but I find that if I focus on the fact that we both want to "make things right" as opposed to thinking that one of us is right and one of us is "wrong," we much more quickly get to a solution that we both agree is right.

Taking a Visible Stand Against Prejudice

A month after 9/11 happened, Kathie Lee Gifford was asked to sing at a concert at the Lincoln Memorial, attended by dignitaries from countries all around the world. I went down to accompany her and to sing a song I had written with Deborah Brevoort called "What Manner of Persons Ought We to Be?" After 9/11, there was a tremendous prejudice among many fearful people against Muslims. Knowing this, Kathie Lee made a it a point to make sure she was photographed arm in arm with a Muslim leader dressed in full Muslim garb. As a person of prominence, she wanted to do her part to curb anxiety and counteract bigotry. This public act, based on the assumption that we all want to make things right, was truly an act of Kindness.

✿ We Can Be Kind to Ourselves ✿

When you find yourself embroiled in a conflict, try making the assumption that everyone is only doing whatever they're doing because they're trying to make things right. No matter how tough or angry or pushy they're being, see them as simply wanting to make things right and watch how the tone of the transaction changes. If we could all understand everyone else's character in this way, we would feel safer and more connected to the world, our choices of thoughts and action would be different, and the world would be a better place.

✿ We Can Be Kind in the World ✿

1. When you are having a problem with someone, try to figure out what it is that *they* want to have made right, and then do everything you can to make it right for them. That is kindness.

2. The next time you're in an upsetting situation, look for the opportunity to show empathy by acknowledging someone else's frustration. Let's say your plane was cancelled, you're on a long line of upset people trying to get their flights rerouted, and everyone is yelling at the service person behind the desk. When you get up to the desk, try starting the conversation by saying, "Wow, this must be a fun day for you!" or something that lets them know that you understand they're trying their best and that it must be difficult for them to have everyone yelling at them. Be the one kind person in the crowd.

3. The next time you're having a fight with someone, try stopping in the middle and saying, "What are we fighting for? We're both good people and there must be a way we can work this out." See what happens when you totally change the tone of the conversation from fighting to kindness.

CHAPTER 14

Does Nobody Want to See It?
Does Nobody Understand?

When we think about this, we often think, "Why would someone not want to see that kindness is something that's available to all of us at all times? Why would someone not choose kindness, and choose instead to attack or have an outburst of anger?" The answers are many: Fear. Shame. Guilt. Mistrust of others and of oneself. Sometimes we think that if we are kind, others will take advantage of us. Sometimes, because of incidents that happened with a particular ethnic or religious group in the past, or even incidents we have heard about in the news or from friends, we make generalizations about everyone in that group. This is what prejudice and bigotry are: "attributing the acts of a single person or small group of individuals to everyone in that group." When we do this, we dehumanize people and in doing so, we dehumanize ourselves. It can be challenging to override the uncomfortable sensations that arise when memories are brought back because someone looks or talks like someone who has harmed us in the past. In such cases, we are often afraid to "take the risk" of seeing this person as an individual rather than as part of a group, but if we are to stop prejudice—in short, if we are to be kind—we must do it. Obviously, looking at the world, it's clear that there is great resistance to letting ourselves see the world through the eyes of kindness. We're always afraid that we'll lose power to the "other" or be taken advantage of. It takes a tremendous amount of trust and faith to be able to make the first move and to maintain kindness no matter what we are seeing in front of us. The simple song "Let There Be Peace on Earth and Let It Begin With Me" reminds us that Peace and Kindness begin inside *each and every one of us*—but so often, practicing this is much harder to actually do than the lyric would suggest.

Don't Assume

Years ago, my mother walked out of her New York apartment building and two teenagers grabbed her purse and ran. She called the police, and in a few minutes a black policeman arrived. When he asked her what had happened, my mother remembers exactly what she said: "I walked out of my building, and two teenage boys of about seventeen or eighteen years of age grabbed my purse and ran." The black policeman asked, "Were the boys Black or Puerto Rican?" The black policeman assumed that the boys had to be one of those two, that they couldn't possibly be White or Asian or anything else. This was completely based on past experiences, but my mother couldn't fail to notice that prejudice against Black people existed among Black people themselves. Although, of course, prejudice from the outside is a real thing, we must be careful not to take on these prejudices and use them against ourselves.

That Was Acting

Chuck Cooper, an extremely talented and well-known black actor, won a Tony Award for playing a vicious, horrible pimp in the Broadway show *The Life*. A while after the run of the play, I was holding auditions for *King Island Christmas*, an oratorio that I had written with my writing partner Deborah Brevoort. Debbie and I were holding the auditions in my home, and we had requested from Chuck's agent that he come over and audition. Neither of us had ever met him. I have to say that frankly, I was nervous about his coming over to my house, as I had experienced his viciousness and his power when I'd seen him on the stage. When the doorbell rang, I opened it and was greeted by a cherubic, smiling man who extended his hand and said, in a delightfully friendly voice, "Hi, I'm Chuck." He must have been used to people who had seen him in *The Life* being taken aback, and I must have visibly shown my surprise—because the next thing he said was, "That was acting." In fact, he was so different from his stage persona that he and my collaborator, Deborah Brevoort, fell in love on the spot and are married today.

🌰 We Can Be Kind to Ourselves 🌰

Whenever you are in a circumstance where you have a preconceived notion of someone, either because of publicity or past experience, see if you can move past that generalized preconception and see the person as an individual. In America, one of the gold standards of our judicial system is "innocent until *proven* guilty." Assume the best about a person. And while you're at it, if you notice that you have judgments about someone else, look inside yourself and see if you have those same judgments about yourself. In these ways, not only are you being kind to yourself, but you are bringing out the most potential for kindness in the other person.

🍂 We Can Be Kind in the World 🍂

1. When you are dealing with someone who has political views opposite to your own, or when you find yourself in a business conflict and the other person is treating you unkindly or attacking you, don't attack back. Treat them with kindness no matter how they're treating you and see what happens.

2. If you see a child or an animal being abused, step in, say something, or, if to step in directly would endanger you, report it. Often people walk right by such situations because they are afraid, even when they have the power to stop it by doing something directly or indirectly. When you spot abuse or extreme unkindness, notice it, see it, and do something.

3. When you encounter prejudice or when someone makes a remark about a particular group of people

that is unkind, uninformed, or bigoted, do not stay silent. Say something. You don't have to say it meanly, but you do have the power to at least bring to light that you feel this is unkind and that the remark does not go unnoticed.

CHAPTER 15

The Power to Heal Is Right Here in Our Hand

If each of us truly understood this, the world would be a completely different place. So many of us spend so much time focusing on what "they" are doing, what's wrong with the world, that we lose sight of the fact that the only thing we have control of is what "we" are doing: how we're acting, how we're responding, what messages we're putting forth into the world. So often, we misguidedly think that the world has to change before we can be OK. The truth is, the physical world is nothing more than a mirror of what we're thinking. When people hear this, they think I'm saying that we are causing things to happen in the world. That's not what I'm saying at all. By mirror, I mean that the only thing we see when we look at any circumstance in the world is our own thoughts. There are people who get rejected and think they must be awful people. There are other people who get rejected and think it must mean that something better is coming along. This is not being a Pollyanna. It just points out that different people see themselves differently and thus see the same circumstances in light of how they see themselves. So if we use every circumstance as a chance to see what we think inside, we can then work on ourselves inside. And when we do that, no matter what we see in the world, we will experience it as a better, kinder place. This is the true and only power we have to heal, and it is truly in our hand.

Let There Be Peace on Earth

I am a member of Unity, a New Thought, Non-Denominational Church. (As a Jewish man I tend to call it Jew-nity, but the point is, you can be any religion and participate in Unity without conflict.) At the end of every service, we would sing a song called "Let There Be Peace on Earth." It took me singing this for about four months until I actually heard the last line: "Let it begin with ME!" Not *them*. Not *you*. Me. What this means is that I'm not waiting for "them" to act correctly before I act correctly. I'm not waiting for "them" to put down their arms before I will put down mine. As I see it, the world is a mirror of what I'm thinking. This doesn't mean that I cause things to happen in the world. It means that when I look at the world, all I really see are my own thoughts about it. It is only when I can change, broaden, modify my own thoughts that I can see the world differently. And when I see the world differently, I not only see myself differently, but the world becomes different. It's crucial that we make the first move, even if we are afraid or doubtful. It's only then that we learn that the power to heal rests truly in our own hands, not in anyone else's. This is true power.

"Let There Be Peace on Earth"
Lyrics and Music by Jill Jackson and Sy Miller

Let there be peace on earth
And let it begin with me;
Let there be peace on earth,
The peace that was meant to be.

With God our Creator
We are family,
Let us walk with each other
In perfect harmony.

Let peace begin with me,
Let this be the moment now;

With every step I take,
Let this be my solemn vow:

To take each moment and live each moment
In peace eternally.
Let there be peace on earth
And let it begin with me.

🌰 We Can Be Kind to Ourselves 🌰

The next time you're in a confrontational or difficult situation where you feel that someone else is doing something to you and you feel that they have to change, ask yourself how you could be different, what you could do to create peace and serenity for yourself and possibly the other person, no matter how hopeless or difficult the situation may seem. It may feel like a big risk, or even futile, to do this. But try it. The shift might be to say nothing when you're dying to say something. To speak kindly when you want to attack. To try to see the other person's point of view. To give in on a point you don't want to give in on. To not retaliate when attacked. Just ask yourself: "How is the power to heal in *my* hands? What can I do to let Peace begin with *me*?" The answer is usually, "Be Kind."

🍫 We Can Be Kind in the World 🍫

1. Physically touching someone you love or someone in need is a way to be kind which many people forget about it. If you're married or in a relationship, a held hand, a rubbed back, a pat on the cheek can mean the world. Hugging a child or family member or pet is one of the most important ways to show them they are loved. Physical affection is a powerful way to show kindness.

2. Often we feel that a political or social problem is too big for us to do anything about. When you encounter such an issue, think: "What is one kind thing I could do that would express a point of view and create a condition where kindness prevails?" Whatever that act is, no matter how small, *do it*. If you're posting on Facebook, try posting kindly. If you're "arguing" with

someone, do it kindly. If you're making a political call, or telling someone you're upset about something, do it kindly.

3. There are many children and many animals who have been abused or treated unkindly. You have the power to do something, ranging from adoption to contributing money, spending time, or publicly advocating. When you see an example of this kind of unkindness, do something. Anything, small or large. Every time you do, you are demonstrating that the power to heal is right here in *your* hand.

WE CAN BE KIND: THE RESOLUTION TO EVERY CONFLICT

"I was once asked why I don't participate in anti-war demonstrations. I said that I will never do that, but as soon as you have a pro-peace rally, I'll be there."
—Mother Teresa

"Human kindness has never weakened the stamina or softened the fiber of a free people. A nation does not have to be cruel to be tough."
—Franklin D. Roosevelt

"You can accomplish by kindness what you cannot accomplish by force."
—Publilius Syrus

"Constant kindness can accomplish much. As the sun makes ice melt, kindness causes misunderstanding, mistrust, and hostility to evaporate."
—Albert Schweitzer

"Kindness is the language which the deaf can hear and the blind can see."
—Mark Twain

"Kindness is no virtue, but a common duty."
—Frederick Greenwood

"A kind act can sometimes be as powerful as a sword."
—Rick Riordan

"Be kind to unkind people—they need it the most."
—Ashleigh Brilliant

"What this world needs is a new kind of army—the army of the kind."
—Cleveland Amory

"The best way to knock the chip off your neighbor's shoulder is to pat him on the back."
—Author Unknown

"Kindness, nobler ever than revenge."
—William Shakespeare

"Other people's actions are the result of their own pain and not the result of any intention to hurt you."
—Thich Nhat Hanh

CHAPTER 16

And It's Not Enough to Talk About It, Not Enough to Sing a Song

So many of us spout the idea that we want peace on earth or that we want people to get along, but our behavior does not demonstrate that. How many times have I admired someone for the things they say in public or the way they are on stage or the principles they espouse in print, and then when I meet them they are unkind or not at all like what they're espousing? How many performers sing songs of love and peace, and then don't behave like that in their own lives? How many politicians spout rhetoric, but in their private lives (or even in the policies they ultimately support) do not at all act in that way? How many religious figures spout values from the pulpit that they themselves do not uphold in their own lives? It's of course good when we speak publicly about being kind, but it's not enough. We actually have to be kind.

Ask Not What Your Country Can Do For You, But What You Can Do For Your Country

A number of years ago, when our small Unity Church in Connecticut seemed to be in trouble, our minister (my partner, Shawn) decided to apply John F. Kennedy's famous inaugural words to the congregation.

Our church had hit a patch where we seemed to be in financial trouble. Rev. Shawn was aware that when a church, or any organization for that matter, hits financial difficulty, it is often because the members of the community have failed to recognize their connectedness and their power. When this happens in a church, it often shows up as a lack of funds, as the congregation not increasing (because when new people come they don't feel welcomed), or as people falling away from the congregation because, in thinking of the church as a place that's supposed to do something for them, they are feeling disappointed. To work on the issues the church was having, Rev. Shawn called a "town meeting" at which the congregation was asked to voice ideas as to how the church could expand, be more fiscally independent, and most of all, function as a community in which the congregation took charge of its own welfare.

There were four parts to this meeting. In the first part, people were asked to take an inventory of what they liked in the church. So that everyone would get a chance to speak, they each had two minutes to list everything the church already had that they liked. When a store takes inventory, it catalogs what it has on the shelves and in storage. It doesn't catalog what it doesn't have. So first, Rev. Shawn wanted a list of what the church had, what was working, what people came to church for. He wrote all these down on a white board so we could all see them.

In the second part, people were asked to voice any complaints they had about the church. There was a very specific way in which they were asked to do this. Rather than complaining, they were asked to list what they would like to see in the church that they didn't see there now. In this way, the comments were made in a positive way that emphasized infinite possibility as opposed to lack. Again, Rev. Shawn wrote down the entire list of things the congregation would like to see in the church.

In the third part, people were asked for suggestions as to how the community might manifest the things the congregation had said they'd like to see. People had a tremendous amount of creative and interesting suggestions as to committees that could be formed, fundraisers that could occur, benefit concerts that could be put on, consciousness-raising workshops, etc.

Rev. Shawn wrote them all down on the board and then turned to the congregation and said, "OK. How are we going to do this?" One member of the congregation gave a diatribe on how a certain committee should be formed and how it should be run. When Rev. Shawn asked her if she was willing to take responsibility for this, she said, "No. I don't have the time." Rev. Shawn's succinct answer was, "If you don't have the time to either do it yourself or see to it that the right people are put together to get it done, we're not interested in your bringing it up." This congregant left the church and has never been back.

But what began to happen as a result of this exchange was that the consciousness of the congregation began to shift from one of "The church has to do things for me" to "This is *my* church; a church is the people in it—not the building, not the minister, but the group of people who form it." The rule became that if you wanted to see something done and brought it up, it was your responsibility to either get it done or to spearhead getting it done by taking responsibility for asking people who could get it done to do it or form a committee to do it. Gradually, people who were not interested in taking this kind of responsibility fell away, and a flock of new people began to show up to join the core group that was willing to not only have ideas but to make them happen.

Today, the church is a thriving, successful, financially viable community of people who feel very connected to each other and are very confident in their ability to, together, make things happen. There is tremendous friendship, passion, and yes, Kindness, among the congregation, as they have learned that it's not enough to talk about it. You have to do it yourself or, in some way, see to it that it gets done.

🖤 We Can Be Kind to Ourselves 🖤

The next time you're in a group situation where you want to see something done, ask yourself: "How could I take responsibility for getting it done?" Whether this means doing it yourself or finding the right people to do it, take it on. This is a tremendous form of kindness to yourself, because you are not only experiencing getting what you want, but even more than that, you're experiencing your power to make it happen. Watch how simply taking on this thought inside yourself changes not only how you feel, but the results you get.

🌫 We Can Be Kind in the World 🌫

1. Put your money where your mouth is. If there is a social cause that concerns you, actively contribute to it with money or time. Don't just rail about it—do something.

2. Whenever you have a complaint about something, turn it into action. Do something to change the condition rather than holding onto it.

3. Always say what you are *for*, not what you're *against*. Do not empower the opposition by talking about how terrible they are. Talk about what you want to see happen, what you believe in. And do something to make it happen.

CHAPTER 17

We Must Walk the Walk About It

How many times have we heard a celebrity, politician, or other public figure come out with a strong anti-drug campaign, only to find out that they themselves have a drug problem? Or learned that someone with vehemently anti-gay views is actually gay themselves? Or discovered that a religious figure publicly promoting celibacy or strong moral laws is personally breaking those very same laws? How many times have we seen politicians make promises in order to get themselves elected, only to see those promises broken or disregarded when they actually get into office? And then, the question becomes, of course: how many times do we do these very kinds of things ourselves? We make promises we either don't intend to keep or intend to keep but forget about later. We project our own problems onto other people and disregard the fact that we have the same problems.

It is one thing to talk about being kind and another thing entirely to actually be kind, especially when the pressures of life come upon us. Although, of course, it's always good to spread the message of kindness, it ultimately does us no good if we do not, in fact, live by that message, even when the going gets rough. It's easy to be kind when everything is going smoothly, but the real proof of the pudding is when we are challenged, attacked, disappointed, or disagreed with, or when we see something that we have judgment about (which often means we have that very same judgment about something in ourselves).

Nazi Germany was a perfect example of this. In Alice Miller's brilliant book *For Your Own Good*, she talks about how a combination of overly strict German child-rearing practices in the early twentieth century and Germany's crushing defeat in World War I created a tremendous self-hatred in many of the German people. This self-hatred became so unbearable that people ended up projecting the hatred outward onto the Jews and other races and creeds that were different from themselves. When a leader came along who told the people that they were better than everyone else, that they were the strongest and the best, and that the hatred they held in their hearts was actually justified, people went along with it and the result was the extermination of six million Jews and six million people of other persuasions, colors, and religions. Kindness went out the window for many people when their own internal feelings of self-hatred and lack of self-worth got too strong to tolerate.

Practicing What You Preach

It is of course much easier to talk about being kind than to actually do it when we're "in the trenches," when something happens that upsets us or that threatens us. My partner is a minister. Now ministers are supposed to set an example, to be upstanding, and to espouse principles and hopefully live them. Of course, so many ministers don't—and often the ones who accuse people of being "sinners" end up being "sinners" themselves. Being intimately acquainted with what my partner goes through, I see firsthand how stressful ministry can be. Every Sunday, no matter how he feels, he gets up and inspires other people, fields their questions, deals with their problems and resistance, etc. As a Spiritual Teacher, he deeply believes in what he's saying, and he "lives" for these Sundays when he can share this with his congregation. But as a human, like any human, he is not immune to the challenges of standing in front of a group of people who expect and need him to hold space for them with such integrity for hours on end. So it's perfectly understandable that after Sunday mornings, he might need to find ways to "let off steam." In the early days of his being a minister, my partner would come home after church and often be "in a mood." And at some point during our interaction, I would find myself saying something like, "You know that spiritual principle you were so eloquently expounding from the pulpit this morning? Well I'm not exactly seeing it in action at the moment." We would actually laugh about it, but he did find it very disturbing that because he was feeling stressed, he was having trouble practicing what he preached. The solution we came to was that after church we would go to lunch. Then I would go home, and he would go back to the church office and take a few hours to unwind and decompress so he could actually practice the kindness he preached about when he got home.

If You Spot It, You Got It!

I've always loved the expression, "If you are pointing a finger at someone else, three fingers are pointing back at you." It gives a clear picture to the concept that when we are finding fault with others, it is very often because we have the fault ourselves. Otherwise, we probably wouldn't be able to spot it.

I have used this concept to great advantage in my teaching. Whenever I am teaching a class, and find myself consistently (and often brilliantly, if I do say so myself) zeroing in on a particular problem my students are having, I immediately go home and look for the same problem in my own work. And invariably, I find it. It is being aware of our own problems that gives us the empathy and kindness to be able to help others with the same problems. Often the best therapists are those who have or have had the same problems as their patients. The best healers are often those who have overcome, or even those who are still working on overcoming, the same issues they're working on healing in their patients. I have observed that the best ministers are usually not those who "pontificate from on high," but those who acknowledge that they have the same issues their congregation has and are using the same tools they're teaching to others to work on their own issues.

When I was twenty years old, I was hospitalized for "panic disorder." Through much hard work and great assistance,

I have learned to conquer this and live a very full life, appearing on Broadway stages, conducting and writing movies and shows, being on television, writing music and books, teaching and lecturing, etc. This doesn't mean that I never experience "panic." I just am used to it. I know what it is and what it will and will not do to me, so it doesn't stop me. Since I have had this experience, I am often asked to work with people who are going through panic disorder. When I work with them, everyone says the same thing: "You can tell in ten seconds if the person who is helping you has actually experienced panic disorder themselves. And it makes all the difference."

One form of kindness, then, is sharing the issues you have and have had in order to help others overcome them. I personally have found this work tremendously gratifying.

Sleep-Out

There's a wonderful organization called Covenant House that gives assistance, shelter, and counseling to homeless teenagers living on the street. A group of actors from the Broadway community decided that they could make a real difference not only in people's awareness but in the contributions Covenant House received if they could recreate the experience of being homeless for people who might not otherwise understand just how challenging it is to be in that condition, especially for a teenager. Each year they stage a sleep-out, where people from the Broadway community and any other folks who might be interested in participating gather together and sleep in the street for the night. There is a great sense of camaraderie in this event, but mostly people are shocked at just how difficult it is to actually spend the night sleeping in the street, even for people who have homes and are just doing it for one night. Sometimes it rains, and there's no way to get out of the rain. Things we take for granted, like the availability of a bathroom when we want one, or having fresh clothes and food at our disposal, are just not there. After doing this for one night, people have a revelation about just how necessary it is to help these kids with donations, volunteerism, and anything else they can think of. This kind act on the part of the organizers in giving people the experience of what these teenagers are going through, and the kind act of the many people who are willing to put themselves through this experience, results in many kind acts by the people who become personally aware of the problem and show their empathy and kindness by spreading the word and giving.

🐑 We Can Be Kind to Ourselves 🐑

There are a number of ways to practice kindness in the area of "walking the walk."

The next time you find yourself upset about something, see if you can "Put Kindness First"—ahead of your need to "express frustration"; ahead of your need to get what you want, possibly at the expense of someone else; ahead of any anger or desperation you might feel. Try making Kindness your number one priority, and watch how situations right themselves and how deeply good and powerful you feel when you do this.

Keep your word. When you say you're going to do something, do it, no matter how difficult it may be.

Watch your projections. When you see yourself criticizing or judging someone else, look to yourself and find the place in yourself that you are judging. Instead of working on the other person, see if you can use the other person as a mirror to work on yourself, which in truth is the only place you can ever really work.

When you see someone in trouble and you want to help, or if you have judgments about them, try walking a mile in their shoes. Try putting yourself in their position: see how it feels, see what you would need if you were actually in that position. This will enable you to give them what they need, because you've found out, inside yourself, what is truly needed.

We Can Be Kind in the World

1. Practice what you preach. If you are against drugs, don't do drugs. If you are anti-smoking, don't smoke. If you are asking students or colleagues or the board of your company or church to do something, make sure you're doing it too. This may seem obvious, but there are so many cases where celebrities who endorse anti-drug programs are caught doing drugs, where preachers who preach against certain kinds of behavior are caught doing the very behavior they condemn, and lawmakers

who make laws for others act as though those laws do not apply to them. If you're going to talk the talk, you have to walk the walk.

2. If you say you're going to do something, do it. No excuses, no procrastination, no rationalizations—*do it!*

3. If you find yourself criticizing a particular group of people or a particular behavior to a great degree, examine yourself and find the places where you think, feel or act like that. Then change your own behavior and refrain from criticizing others. What we see in other people is really nothing more than our own thoughts. Fix the things in yourself that you think of as wrong in other people, and the world will be a kinder place.

CHAPTER 18

You and I, Do or Die, We've Got To Try to Get Along

Getting along and being kind can be hard work. In order to do it, we have to make a conscious effort to own our own thoughts and sensations, to see ourselves as related to other people, and to be willing to treat everyone with the same kindness with which we wish to be treated. This sounds like a nice idea, but in times of stress we can forget and act out. Not only that, but in times of stress the whole world can forget and act out, causing wars, killing, starvation, discrimination, and other truly life-and-death situations. So being kind is not just something that's nice to think about and do occasionally. The survival of our planet and the well-being of all its inhabitants depends on it.

Kindness Is the Reason I'm Here Today

In the very early 1900s, my grandmother was a young Jewish girl living in Russia. She was twelve years old and was staying in an inn owned by a Christian woman. Now at that time, there were attacks known as pogroms where Cossacks would come into towns armed with guns and swords and massacre Jews and people of other races and religions that they found undesirable. Early one morning, a group of Cossacks burst into the inn where my twelve-year-old grandmother was staying, brandished their guns and knives, and said to the innkeeper, "Are there any Jews staying here? If there are, give them to us!" The Christian innkeeper, who knew very well that my grandmother was there, and also knew very well that my grandmother was Jewish, picked up a cross, held it in front of her, and said, "I swear by this cross, there are no Jews in this inn!" The Cossacks left, and my grandmother's life was saved. When my grandmother told me this story many years ago, I realized that had this Christian woman not done that act of kindness that took so much courage, I would not be here today.

❧ We Can Be Kind to Ourselves ❧

Take on the thought that there is a way to get along with everyone, no matter what your differences might be. In this way, you are being kind to yourself, because you are opening yourself to a world of possibilities, no matter what the circumstances. Watch how creative solutions you may have never imagined come out of this kind of mindset.

❧ We Can Be Kind in the World ❧

1. When you're discussing a controversial topic in a group, rather than constantly trying to push your agenda, *listen*. Open your mind to other points of view; refrain from arguing with the other person before really taking in their point of view. Do not interrupt while they are talking. Let them know they have a point, even if you don't agree with them.

2. When you disagree with someone or are in conflict with them, ask yourself: "How important is it?" Sometimes it is important, but sometimes it's more important to keep the peace and allow the other person to win a

point. Ask yourself in each situation: "What is the kindest thing I can do here?"

3. The fourth definition of the word "romance" in the dictionary is, "Not true. Made up." I've always loved this. Romance is something you do, something you create, rather than being something that you have to feel a certain way at a certain moment to produce. So light the candles, serve a nice dinner, act in a loving manner toward someone you love whether or not you feel it at that particular moment. Shut your mouth if you think it will ruin the mood. (It's often said that the key to a good marriage is to communicate fully, but I have found that the key to a good marriage is sometimes to know when to shut your mouth!) You create the tone of your relationship, and since it's a relationship that you are in, you get to make it better by setting a tone of kindness.

WE CAN BE KIND: AN ACTION WE MUST ALWAYS TAKE

"A tree is known by its fruit; a man by his deeds. A good deed is never lost; he who sows courtesy reaps friendship, and he who plants kindness gathers love."
—**Saint Basil**

"The really fantastic thing about kindness is that it's free.... It's the thing that brings us all together."
—**Lady Gaga**

"Extend yourself in kindness....Ask the universe, 'How can I be used for a purpose that is greater than myself?'"
—**Oprah Winfrey**

"World peace must develop from inner peace. Peace is not just mere absence of violence. Peace is, I think, the manifestation of human compassion."
—Dalai Lama

"Carry out a random act of kindness, with no expectation of reward, safe in the knowledge that one day someone might do the same for you."
—Princess Diana

"How wonderful it is that nobody need wait a single minute before starting to improve the world."
—Anne Frank

"The simplest acts of kindness are by far more powerful than a thousand heads bowing in prayer."
—Mahatma Ghandi

"When we give cheerfully and accept gratefully, everyone is blessed."
—Maya Angelou

"The smallest act of kindness is worth more than the greatest intention."
—Khalil Gibran

"I will speak ill of no man…and will speak all the good I know of everybody."
—Benjamin Franklin

"Life is short but there is always time for courtesy."
—Ralph Waldo Emerson

"It's nice to be important, but it's more important to be nice."
—Author Unknown

CHAPTER 19

And Maybe We'll Find True Peace of Mind

So many people think that true peace of mind can be found outside themselves: in possessions, in power, in money. But if we ask ourselves, "Why do we want these things?" the answers always come back: "To have security, to have a feeling of safety, to have a feeling of personal power, and, in short, to have peace of mind." The things we really want are all internal experiences, and yet so many of us keep seeking them in external "things." The external "things" that we want, which we think will get us the internal "experiences" we desire, are actually, in and of themselves, meaningless. How many celebrities or extremely wealthy people have we seen who are far from happy and serene?

So we must ask ourselves, "What is true peace of mind?" Knowing we're loved. Knowing we're safe. Knowing we're good. Loving and caring for ourselves and others, and knowing that others love and care for us. Knowing that the abundance of the universe is always available. Sometimes we forget that the first step in Kindness can be to be kind to ourselves. To give ourselves a break. To not shame ourselves or think less of ourselves. Only when we can know that the source of peace of mind is within ourselves can we offer kindness to others.

I'm Destitute

Years ago I was at a dinner party, and there was a woman at the table who was going through an extremely messy divorce. She was really hating her husband, and at one point she said, "That creep has left me completely destitute! He has taken everything except the apartment, and I have to sell it to live! I have nothing! I'm destitute!" When I asked her, "How much are you asking for the apartment?" she said, "$7,775,000!" My first thought was, "Oh, tsk, tsk, this poor woman is down to her last seven million dollars. How will she ever live?" (I hope you can "hear" the sarcasm in these words.) I thought, "How ridiculous and selfish that this woman thinks she's destitute because she's only got a seven-million-dollar apartment. How many people are there who have trouble putting food on the table and yet don't consider themselves destitute and have the ability to be content, happy, and hopeful?" But when I thought about it further, I thought, "Wow. How empty must she feel inside—how lonely, how hopeless—to be able to look at seven million dollars and consider herself destitute?" This woman may have had money and a wealthy lifestyle, but what she didn't have in her life, either coming to her or coming from her, was kindness. Her husband was leaving her, and she was feeling nothing but anger and resentment toward him— and inflicting punishment on herself in thinking of herself as destitute. All the money in the world doesn't make up for kindness.

Forgiveness

I don't think we can have any serious discussion of Kindness without also discussing Forgiveness. They go hand in hand. Forgiveness is an often-misunderstood concept. First of all, as odd as it may seem, Forgiveness has nothing to do with condoning or forgetting a perceived wrong that has been done to us. In fact, Forgiveness is not for the other person. Forgiveness is for ourselves. When we forgive, we accept that something has happened. We notice all the thoughts and sensations we have around it and allow them to be as they are. When we can do this, we release ourselves from bondage and are free to continue our lives without being held back by feelings of resentment, guilt, or shame. I've always loved the expression, "Holding a grudge is like taking poison and hoping the other person dies." In holding resentment, we only damage ourselves. Usually the other person doesn't even know we're holding it and is unaffected by it. And what good would it do for us to have them be upset by it? The only thing that helps us is to forgive.

Years ago, I heard a story of Forgiveness that, although most likely apocryphal, still holds up as a parable. A woman from a wealthy New York family had a son who was about to go to Harvard to study medicine. A few months before he was set to go, he was murdered by a boy his age. During the course of the ensuing investigation, the woman found out that the boy who had murdered her son had come from an extremely dysfunctional poor family, and that abuse and drugs had been a big part of his life. At some point, she realized that even if this boy were convicted and sent to the electric chair, this would not bring her son back or do anything to ease her sense of pain and loss. How many people fight for years to see someone who has murdered a family member of theirs "fry in the electric chair," only to find that when that finally happens they have no sense of peace? Their loss is still there. So this woman performed an act of Forgiveness that would seem impossible for most of us. She dropped the charges and paid for this boy to have the education her son would have had. By forgiving, she didn't bring her son back, but she was able to experience some of the feelings of pride, joy, and love she would have experienced, had she seen her son succeed. More than letting her son's murderer off the hook, she was letting herself off the hook. In this, she was being Kind not only to the boy, but even more so, to herself.

🍃 We Can Be Kind to Ourselves 🍃

The next time you find yourself in a situation where you feel you are lacking something in the "outside" world, whether it be something material or a relationship or money or some kind of success, see if you can get under that sense of lack and look for what it is you're really lacking, inside.

Look for where kindness might be what's lacking. And when you find the answer to that question, try doing the following: First, treat yourself with kindness by opening up to the possibilities that *must* exist in the situation, since infinite possibilities *always* exist, even when we can't see them. Whatever the problem, there are always all sorts ways it can be solved, many of which you may not even have thought of. Next, see if you can look at whoever or whatever you may think is the source of your problem and offer them kindness. This can be the hardest thing to do. In many cases, it's too difficult to offer kindness directly, but at least try to think of them with kindness. The object here is your own serenity and your own sense of peace of mind, no matter what the circumstances. Take a chance and see how kindness can bring about these things which, really, in the end, are all we're after.

We Can Be Kind in the World

1. When you find yourself in conflict, ask yourself: "What action will bring me the most serenity and peace of mind right now?" and take that action. This is different from asking, "How can I win this? How can I be right?"

This is about your peace of mind. And sometimes the action you take will not make you win, but it will give you peace of mind. All we really want is peace of mind. When we have that, nothing else matters and everything falls into place.

2. When you're in a relationship or in a conflict, look at the other person and ask yourself: "What do I think will give them true peace of mind?" And see if you can give it to them, either completely or as much as possible. This is kindness, and often as you give it you will receive it.

3. Do kind things for yourself. In the middle of the greatest times of pressure or conflict, take a break, take a nap, call a friend, go to a movie, or have a nice dinner. Even if it's counterintuitive, do it. And if the thing that would give you the most peace of mind is to keep working, to push through, do that. Be kind to yourself, whatever that means.

CHAPTER 20

If We Always Remember, We Can Be Kind

Again, the operative word here is *always*. It's easy to be kind when circumstances are easy, when we agree with other people, when we feel strong and empowered and feel like we have something to give. But the real challenge is to be kind all the time. Like gratitude, kindness is something we must *always* practice, no matter what the circumstances, no matter how we feel. And when we can do this, the world will change before our eyes. Because no matter what, no matter how powerless we might feel, there is something that is *always* within our power—we can *always* be *kind*.

❧ We Can Be Kind to Ourselves ❧

You've read this book, and hopefully some of the stories and examples of kindness I've related have touched you or have stimulated you to think about kindness. The best way to practice kindness is, in *every* situation—good, bad, upsetting, happy, competitive, hopeless, frightening, angering—to pause for a moment and ask yourself: "How can I be kind here?" What a different world it would be, if we could just do that.

🍫 Practicing Kindness in the World 🍫

1. Choose kindness.

2. Choose kindness.

3. Choose kindness.

"WE CAN BE KIND" WHEN WE WANT PEACE OF MIND

"A kind and compassionate act is often its own reward."
—**William John Bennett**

"The fragrance always stays in the hand that gives the rose."
—**Hada Bejar**

"There is overwhelming evidence that the higher the level of self-esteem, the more likely one will be to treat others with respect, kindness, and generosity."
—**Nathaniel Branden**

"Kindness can become its own motive. We are made kind by being kind."
—**Eric Hoffer**

"Kindness is twice blessed. It blesses the one who gives it with a sense of his or her own capacity to love, and the person who receives it with a sense of the beneficence of the universe."
—Dawna Markova

"When we practice loving-kindness and compassion we are the first ones to profit."
—Rumi

"Kindness is an inner desire that makes us want to do good things even if we do not get anything in return. It is the joy of our life to do them. When we do good things from this inner desire, there is kindness in everything we think, say, want and do."
—Emanuel Swedenborg

"When we feel love and kindness toward others, it not only makes others feel loved and cared for, but it helps us also to develop inner happiness and peace."
—The 14th Dalai Lama

"Kindness is the golden chain by which society is bound together."
—Goethe

"Kindness makes a fellow feel good whether it's being done to him or by him."
—**Frank A. Clark**

"Kindness holds the key to the secret of our own transformation and, in the process, of the transformation of the world."
—**Jean Maalouf**

"Without kindness, there can be no true joy."
—**Thomas Carlisle**

Epilogue

As a songwriter, I understand that songs do not come from me, but rather through me from some universal source to which I open my heart and mind. As such, I am not always aware of all of the meanings the song might have. Different singers often bring out meanings I never thought of.

In writing this book and examining and thinking about each line of my song, my own understanding of not only what the song is saying but of Kindness itself has been greatly expanded.

I have come to understand that Kindness is more than being nice. Kindness is more than being polite. Kindness is more than manners, or being sweet. Kindness is more than how we act and what we do. Kindness is a deeply pervasive and powerful way of being, a way of looking at people and the world. Kindness is looking past appearances and into the heart and soul of who people really are underneath all that. Kindness is looking at circumstances and knowing, without a doubt, that there are solutions and possibilities in even the most hopeless situations. Kindness is not only about how we think of and act toward others. It is, perhaps most importantly, how we think of and act toward ourselves.

I hope that in listening to this song and reading this book and the stories it contains, you have come to a greater understanding of the far-reaching ramifications and meaning of Kindness, and that you are inspired to practice it in new and life-changing ways.

I would love to hear from you as to how Kindness has played out in your life. If you are so inclined, please email your stories to me MIDDER2000@aol.com.

My hope is that listening to this song and reading this book will enrich your life with Kindness as much as writing them has enriched mine.

Authors bio

David Friedman

David Friedman, one of this country's most beloved songwriters, is best known for writing songs that touch our hearts and speak to our souls. He has written songs for everyone from Disney to Diana Ross, produced all of the late, great Nancy LaMott's CDs and wrote many of her best-known songs, conducted and arranged vocals for six musicals on Broadway and numerous Disney animated films (including *Beauty and the Beast, Aladdin, Pocahontas,* and *The Hunchback of Notre Dame*), has written songs for The *Lizzie McGuire Movie, Aladdin* and *the King of Thieves,* and *Bambi II* and *Trick,* scored three television series, cowrote the family musical celebration, *King Island Christmas* (with Deborah Brevoort), the musical *Scandalous* (with Kathie Lee Gifford and David Pomeranz), which played on Broadway in 2012, has performed his revue, *Listen To My Heart: The Songs of David Friedman* for audiences Off-Broadway, all over America and abroad, and wrote the music to the hit musical, *Desperate Measures* (with Peter

Kellogg). He currently has three other new musicals in the works and ready to go, and is in his eighth year of writing and performing a "song-a-month" for the Today Show's "Everyone Has a Story" segment. In an effort to give back some of the lessons he's learned in his fulfilling and varied career, David has written a groundbreaking book called The Thought Exchange: Overcoming Our Resistance to Living a Sensational Life and a sequel to that book called The Healing Power of "Negative" Thoughts and "Uncomfortable" Sensations. David lectures and teaches all over the United States. For more information, go to MIDDERMusic.com.

Nancy LaMott

Nancy LaMott, one of the greatest interpreters of popular American Standards of her generation, was the first to record "We Can Be Kind." Even more than twenty years after her untimely passing at the age of forty-three, her recording of this song remains iconic. In her brief but powerfully influential career, Nancy not only recorded legendary versions of David Friedman songs such as "Listen to My Heart," "Help Is on the Way," and "We

Live on Borrowed Time," but also put her distinctive mark on many classic standards as well as songs written by contemporary songwriters.